POLICY AND PF

NU

SCHOOL LEADERSHIP

POLICY AND PRACTICE IN EDUCATION

POLICY AND PRACTICE IN EDUCATION
SERIES EDITORS
JIM O'BRIEN and CHRISTINE FORDE

SCHOOL LEADERSHIP

Second Edition

Jim O'Brien
Dean, Moray House School of Education,
University of Edinburgh

Janet Draper
Head of Department and Professor of Educational Studies
Hong Kong Baptist University

Daniel Murphy
Headteacher, Lornshill Academy, Alloa
Formerly Director of the
Centre for Educational Leadership,
University of Edinburgh

DUNEDIN

Published by
Dunedin Academic Press Ltd
Hudson House
8 Albany Street
Edinburgh EH1 3QB
Scotland

ISBN: 978-1-903765-93-7
ISSN 1479-6910

First edition 2003
Reprinted 2006, 2007
Second edition 2008
Reprinted 2010, 2011

British Library Cataloguing in Publication data
A catalogue record for this book is available from the British Library

Typeset by Makar Publishing Production
Printed and bound in Great Britain by CPI Antony Rowe

CONTENTS

SERIES EDITORS' INTRODUCTION

A second edition of *School Leadership* is timely, given the significant changes in education since the publication of the first edition in 2003. There has been a shift in educational policy in Scotland, as elsewhere in the UK, away from a focus on 'management' to a concentration on 'leadership'. This book traces the development of thinking around these two issues and explores the implications for the practice and development of leaders in school. The book draws widely from work undertaken in Scotland particularly in leadership development and sets the emerging issues in the context of wider scholarship on leadership. We now talk of 'the leadership agenda' and 'leadership at all levels'. Thus the authors explore school leadership in the wider context of leadership of education at national and local governmental levels and this discussion helps highlight some of the tensions experienced by headteachers. A particular strength of this book is its use of the experiences of those leading schools today to illuminate these challenges.

Dr Jim O'Brien
Dean and Director,
Moray House School of Education,
The University of Edinburgh

Christine Forde
Professor of Leadership & Professional
Learning, Department of Educational
Studies, Faculty of Education,
The University of Glasgow

ACKNOWLEDGEMENTS

The preparation and revision of a book depends on the goodwill and support of many people. In the past few years, the professional partnership between the university, local authority staff, teachers and headteachers has contributed greatly to our developing understanding. We should like to thank many colleagues in the Moray House School of Education for the free exchange of ideas that have helped us develop and shape our current position, in particular, past and current colleagues in the Centre for Educational Leadership in the University of Edinburgh, Jim Fleming, Jennifer Kerr, Eric Melvin, Deirdre Torrance, Graham Thomson and Mike Cowie. Additionally, involvement in the national leadership strategy group and the group involved in writing for Scotland the OECD country report on leadership has meant exposure to a further range of key personnel and ideas which have helped to shape our thinking.

INTRODUCTION

This short volume aims to explore current issues in school leadership, in the context of state schooling in general, and Scottish schooling in particular. It will not produce definitive or tightly argued answers but some broad themes are discernible. Consider these questions:

When was the last time you were 'led' by someone else?

Do you enjoy the experience of being led?

Did you want to be 'led'?

When was the last time someone 'followed' you?

Is it more or less likely that another person would 'follow' your lead if you exercised power over them, or if you tried to influence them, or if you worked alongside them?

In a work context, do you accept leadership from those with power over you, or do you resent it?

If, as for many, you sometimes accept and sometimes resent, what makes the difference?

In the choices you make in your life away from work, are you 'led'?
– in matters of consumer choice – for example, by fashion, by design, by peer influence? or
– in matters of politics, for example, by the media, by party, by the ideas of others?

Are there any work, leisure or personal relationships of which the following are true:
– you always lead?
– you always follow?
– you sometimes lead, sometimes follow and sometimes seek agreement on the best way forward?

We begin with these questions about how we, as individuals living in a democratic society, conceive of leadership. The questions are straightforward, but your answers may open up some of the complexity of this important concept.

The English language has a variety of pejorative expressions for the experience of being led, and for those who enjoy being led. We talk of being 'led by the nose', of following 'like sheep'. Buried deep within our modern understanding of what it means to be an adult person in a democracy is a feeling that we should make free choices, independently, ourselves. In Scotland, a suspicion of those who seek to lead, those who think they are 'better', or who behave as if they have more to offer, is summed up in the saying, 'Ah kent his faither', reminding the listener that the (male) person involved is from the same background and should not think himself in any way special. Yet in the world of business and public service, the importance of 'leadership' is emphasized everywhere ... and hidden behind leaders there are followers (Thody, 2000). A global publishing industry flourishes with myriad texts on different approaches to leadership and what makes a good or effective leader. Literature abounds on leadership styles and behaviours and what leaders must do. Companies spend huge sums of money on recruiting and training the people they think will make a difference to their performance. The charismatic approaches of successful business leaders who have turned multi-national companies around in high profile ways are held up as exemplars alongside and in contrast to those others who inspire followers through their values or way of life, including, occasionally, political leaders. No matter the nature of their behaviour or authority, leaders clearly lead only because others follow.

Our understanding of leadership practice is further complicated if the purposes leadership should serve, in a particular context, are unclear, or contested. In some situations such as warfare or antagonistic politics, leadership purpose may be clearly defined. In the case of schooling, purpose is seldom so clear. Contested conceptions of the purposes of schooling inform the literature of school leadership: some, for example favouring effectiveness of schooling as measured by exam performance of students, over, for example, the clarity of the moral message which the school projects. In recent times, published national priorities for Scottish schools outline, for example, a wider set of school functions, well beyond the development in their pupils of a functional competence in key skills. The five national priorities were grouped under the headings of:

Achievement and Attainment
Framework for Learning
Inclusion and Equality
Values and Citizenship
Learning for Life.

These national priorities are now encompassed in a new approach to the curriculum in Scotland, 'A Curriculum for Excellence' (see A Curriculum for Excellence, online), that is currently being developed and introduced.

Leadership to achieve these kinds of broad aims will require more than technical skills in pedagogy or efficient resource management. Chapter 1 therefore sets a wider context within which discussion about schooling and its purposes can be set.

The literature on leadership generally has been written to inspire and motivate those in leadership positions, or those who aspire to them. This is as true of school leadership as it is of more general theories of leadership, discussed further in Chapter 2. Such literature is aimed at, and tends only to be read by, those aspiring to be leaders, not by those who are led. The concept of leadership presented is almost invariably a positive one. This is true both in the inspirational literature which narrates or analyses the importance of leaders and how they have made a difference for good in the lives of others, and in the more prosaic training literature that describes good leadership practice and highlights the desirable qualities and skills of the successful leader. Yet, without initial reference to that literature, we have established with a short set of simple questions that the experiences of leadership, of being led and of making decisions with others collectively, are complex. They tie into our sense of personal identity and into our understanding of democratic values and processes. We cannot take 'leadership' to be an uncontested good.

We also know that the experience of school leadership, as described by those involved in leading, those who aspire to lead and those who do not want to lead, is not at all clear and certain and we will review this in Chapter 3. It can be a painful experience, with a great deal of stress or personal hurt. It may place unreasonable demands on those closest to the aspirant 'leader'. It may involve mixed motives – from a desire to serve to a desire for power. This emotional and functional intricacy, and the uncertainty and tensions associated with it, are necessary outcomes of the complexity of leadership as a concept and of the contested character of schooling as a social process.

Partiality also affects research into school leadership and may influence the preparation and support for school leaders. We review provision for the preparation and support of school leaders particularly headteachers in Chapter 4. Gunter (2001) summarised research within a frame that considers the viewpoint from which research is conducted. When school leadership, for example, is described in one of the burgeoning texts used on headship training programmes, what presumptions about leadership have underpinned research designs? Has headship been equated conceptually with school leadership? Has the author considered other levels of leadership within schools? These and other questions suggest further aspects of complexity in defining and discussing leadership in schools, and in Chapter 5 we reflect on developments since 2003 when the first edition of this book was published and look ahead and anticipate the next steps necessary if we are further to develop our understanding and practice of leadership.

Although many of the examples of the study are chosen from the Scottish system, many of the issues raised have a more general application and we have illustrated issues with international commentary and research.

CHAPTER 1

LEADERSHIP, SOCIETY AND SCHOOLING

Schooling and democratic society

To understand school leadership, we need to understand schools. We therefore in this chapter will situate school leadership within the broad set of political and social factors that frame schools and schooling. In the context of democratic living we are uneasy about the concept of leadership. We give power and influence to leaders, but are keen to keep them in check. Clearly there are complex connections between our concept of democracy, current structures for democratic participation and the sharing and distribution of power, and the ways in which schools work, and what we expect of them. We will also offer a brief account of some of the framing experiences of the past twenty or so years which have influenced decisions and decision-making in Scottish schools and outline different ways of looking at schools – 'outside in and inside out' – which correspond in some ways to two different ways of framing schools as organisations. Scotland, in line with many democratic societies, has protected freedoms to establish and run schools separately from the state, and while some aspects of school leadership are shared across every kind of school, the management of state schools through elected representatives provides a very different framing context for school leadership within these schools. While some of the following discussion is relevant to all schools, much is of singular relevance to those schools provided by the state as a public service.

There is a tension, and suspicion, in democratic societies about the existence and powers of leaders. Control of the power of the state which should exercise its authority only with the consent of those governed, and of those leaders who exercise that power, has been an enduring theme in the development of modern democratic societies since the US Declaration of Independence. It is an ideal which has underpinned some of the most significant political struggles of our age, from the war against Hitler to the liberation struggles of colonised peoples.

Moving from the broad brush of political ideals to the detail of what the modern, increasingly complex state does, it is harder to follow these ideas of freedom and consent through into practice. The modern state, with its wide-ranging powers and resources to shape experiences and opportunities, has a detailed involvement with individuals in many aspects of their lives, education not least. One of the primary mechanisms for ensuring educational opportunity and experience is through schooling, and every modern state had developed education as a public service, and as a compulsory experience, through schools. Lindsay Paterson, in an earlier volume in this series (Paterson, 2000a) outlines five main themes of modern public education, characteristic of Scotland and of many other state education systems in Europe and elsewhere. He makes significant distinctions between the Scottish experience, with these international parallels, and the more distinctive and unusual English experience, outlined for example in Carr's strong critique of the educational reforms of the 1980s and 1990s (Carr and Hartnett, 1996).

The common themes Paterson identifies can be summarised:

- Education has been built up by the state.
- Education systems shape personal identity.
- In recent times there has been an increasing assertion of the individual through consumerist models, which are part of a complex set of social developments.
- There is tension between the state and 'civil society', those connections, relationships, organisations and activities which exist within society but are not controlled by the state.
- Mass education both followed and supported mass democracy in a continually expanding model of educational opportunity and experience, although democracy has largely been a democracy of voters, as government has exercised power, once elected, through a technocracy of experts.

In a modern democratic society such as Scotland, we cannot then examine schools, and school leadership, without giving proper consideration to the political context of publicly funded schooling. In the Scottish system of publicly funded schools, it is now an expectation that schools are not just provided and held accountable through a democratic process, but themselves contribute to democratic formation. National guidance on citizenship education reinforced by the inclusion of democratic formation and citizenship in the National Priorities in 2002 has now become a central element of the new Scottish 'Curriculum for Excellence' which seeks to ensure that all Scottish young people become 'responsible citizens'.

Schools then are provided for the people, by the state, yet the systems established to ensure that they operate efficiently and effectively can present the school as an agency of control rather than an empowering education service. The tension between empowerment and control, as realised in the provision of education through publicly funded schools, can be illustrated for the purposes of this study by looking at schools through two different lenses – 'inside out' and 'outside in'. Another popular image follows lines of power, influence and control: 'bottom–up' or 'top–down'. This is not to provide a tight sociological framing, but a way into viewing the complexity of the issues at play.

Scottish schools and the state – the recent story

The particular relationship between state and schooling developed in Scotland alongside the adoption of universalist welfare values in school education since 1945 has been analysed sociologically and historically in a number of important studies (McPherson and Raab, 1988; Humes, 1986; Paterson, 2000a; Paterson, 2000b). This relationship involved:

- an extensive 'managed' centralisation, in which many of the lines of power and control lay hidden behind national 'guidance', and/ or national Quangos or agencies such as the Scottish Consultative Council on the Curriculum, the Scottish Qualifications Authority and Her Majesty's Inspectors of Schools;
- a separation between strategic policy (national government) and provision (local authorities) which meant that neither local nor national government saw itself as responsible for failures in policy or in implementation, in relation to the curriculum, the structure of schooling or the structure of the teaching profession;
- a limited, and limiting, model of teacher professionalism in which the teacher's job was conceived as being that of an employee responsible for implementing policy decided elsewhere.

This is a crucial relationship within which to frame a discussion of school leadership. Leadership implies a capacity to make decisions, to set a direction with and for a group of people. But who does decide what happens in Scottish schools? Is it or should it be the employers? Is it or should it be the government? Is it or should it be the teachers? Is it or should it be the headteacher? Is it or should it be the pupils or parents? The many disputes over the past twenty or thirty yeas between the teaching profession and the government of the day in relation to national policy direction, and between the teaching profession and their employers in local authorities in relation to pay and conditions of service clearly show the struggle for power and control between these different key players.

In the 1990s a simplistic managerialist mindset lay behind a series of reforms, led by national government, aimed at transforming educational practice and designed to make the teaching profession more accountable (and, so the thinking went, schools would therefore be more effective) through greater control:

- Tight curriculum guidance was reinforced by an Inspection system looking for compliance.
- Staff appraisal was introduced.
- National testing in primary schools and the reporting of public examination results in public 'league tables' began.
- Self-evaluation against nationally identified indicators of best performance and systematic development planning using a 'management by objectives' model were encouraged.
- Opportunities were offered for parents to become involved in school governance through School Boards (with an option to opt out of local authority control altogether).

The accountability agenda within public service was one of the flagship policies of the new liberalism that swept through all public services in the United Kingdom, and education among other services in many developed economies. The development of this new managerialism in education is summarised in Gronn's outstanding analysis of changing work patterns among those involved in educational leadership (Gronn, 2003).

In Scotland, these developments took a specific form. Scottish civic society (Paterson, 2000a) exercised greater power, from the base of a strong civic consensus against the wholesale 'marketisation' of public schooling. An important example is the campaign by the Educational Institute of Scotland (EIS), Scotland's leading teachers' association, against national testing in the early 1990s. A range of civic organisations, including parent groups, trade unions and political parties were marshalled by the EIS to resist the imposition of a primary school testing regime which might lead to 'league tables' of primary schools. Another albeit more indirect example lies in the fact that only two out of almost 4,000 Scottish schools chose to 'opt out' of local authority control under the powers given to School Boards. In both these cases, the 'opt out' was at least in part to resist the threat of school closure.

Despite unpromising contextual factors in terms of the profession, school structures, the financial constraints of tight public spending rounds throughout the 1980s and 1990s and a managerialist mindset on the part of politicians and some senior officials, the ideals of public schooling as a force for good remained strong. Ideals to which both the teaching profession and their employers signed up – to equalise opportunity and to counter disadvantage – acted as a dynamic intellectual force for change and development, requiring schools and policy makers to examine and reform practice. Moreover these ideals had given a strong and coherent sense of professional identity to many of the teaching cohort who had entered the profession in the early 1970s and were moving into influential positions in the 1990s. Their optimism about education, their commitment to the values of public schooling and their determination to resist what they saw as the excessive marketisation of school education characteristic of educational reform in England during this period, led them to modify and customise politically inspired educational reform. The 'Scottish model', behind the tensions and conflicts of this era, therefore saw a steady continuation of trends in widening educational opportunity, evidenced in enhanced stay-on rates, improved examination results, and wider access to Higher and Further Education beyond school (Paterson, 2000a, p. 47).

However, Scottish schools, particularly secondary schools, were on the whole becoming more 'managed' and less spontaneous. A key indicator of this, as already mentioned above, was the significant reduction in the provision of 'extracurricular activities' as a result of the 'work to rule' of 1985–6. More and more of the experiences of pupils of school became the experiences of the classroom alone. The Standard Grade curriculum for those aged 14–16, and its planned successor for those aged 16–18, Higher Still, consisted of technically complex courses with sophisticated assessment systems, demanding more of teachers' time. Pupils had to write well to do well. Schools were professionally defined increasingly by assessed formal classroom experiences and less as communities of learning, which might offer diverse experiences and avenues to personal growth.

After the election of a new government in 1997, the devolution of power to a Scottish parliament based in Edinburgh in 1999, and subsequent legislation (SEED, 2000a) to establish a set of national priorities for Scottish education, the climate within which schools operate has changed again. A new and more positive set of circumstances has been created. Increased funding allocations to schools have paralleled a clear commitment to local empowerment and an expectation that schools will involve local communities, particularly the young people themselves, in decisions about the school. Rather than education being something organised by national government and delivered to the people by teachers, education was re-conceptualised, at least in some quarters, as a process in which local school communities engage with a national agenda for public service in different creative ways. Evidence for this could be found, for example, in the design of the New Community Schools Initiative (Scottish Office, 1998) involving local solutions and creativity rather than national prescription. National priorities for education were specified, widening ambition beyond academic attainment, into areas such as 'values and citizenship' and 'inclusion and equality'. In addition, both within existing primary schools, and in separate nursery schools, the exceptional growth of pre-school education funded by the state has introduced a new element into publicly funded education, paralleled by investment and experiment in early intervention schemes. There has been an increased emphasis on the emotional development of the whole child and less on the acquisition and progression of formal cognitive skills (Jamieson, 2002).

These trends came together in the publication of national guidance on a new kind of curriculum for Scottish education, 'A Curriculum for Excellence' (see online). This goes well beyond previous curricular advice in this area, offering an open-ended challenge, rather than prescribing cognitive outcomes. Scottish schools are now expected to judge the success of the school experience by the extent to which the pupils leaving school display certain key characteristics. Schools are encouraged under this new guidance to seek creative and engaging ways of educating young people to become 'successful learners, confident individuals, active contributors and responsible citizens'. However, although the broad thrust of this new guidance has been well received, worries have emerged about what this will mean in practice, particularly since so many of the building blocks of the old curriculum, including the current national examination structure, remain in place. Meantime, the election of a new government in Scotland, with a different agenda for education has led to further uncertainty over strategic policy.

It is clear, however, that the national forum provided by the new Scottish Parliament has allowed investigation and public debate of educational issues well beyond what was possible before (Paterson, 2000b; and for a sample debate, see Scottish Parliament, 2008). In this changing and contested political landscape, who will 'lead' our discussions about the development of schools? Who will 'lead' the schools? Who has power and influence?

Organisational structures and decision-making powers in Scottish schools

We have summarised the historical and political context through which the contemporary Scottish school has evolved to explain the context and to aid understanding of the complexities, compromises and cultural tensions of the contemporary school. In this section, we offer two viewpoints on schools as organisations – schools as efficient parts of a public service bureaucracy, concerned to deliver initiatives planned at the centre, and schools as organic plural communities, constructing their own understanding of purpose and value. These two viewpoints offer a way into the tensions experienced by the competing lines of force and influence on the school, and the complexity of the leadership issues which result.

As organisations, Scottish schools share many features of classic Weberian bureaucracy – designed for certainty and functional effectiveness, through secure description of role and function and an elaborated division of labour and accountability across the different workers within the organisation. Weber's picture is of a modern world in which the 'iron cage' of rational/mechanical/technical/expert 'bureaucratisation' increasingly stifles the individual. As the state becomes increasingly efficient at providing education (but also other services) through bureaucratic processes, in which technical experts work within a mechanically ordered system, with limited and reducing room for discretion, there is less and less opportunity for the individual to find expression or to create meaning. This picture (summarised in Samier, 2002) suggests that bureaucracy's concern for order, systems, hierarchies, accountability and prescription can stultify creativity and reduce ownership. Bureaucracy is concerned with managing efficiently, not questioning and creating. In the worst case, bureaucracy forgets the purposes for which it has been established and exists to serve its own ends. This is an especially dangerous trend for education, where questioning, critique and the examination of purposes and values, is an essential part of the enterprise.

For much of the past thirty years, the bureaucratic organisational design of the Scottish school has largely been specified nationally by negotiations conducted through the Scottish Joint Negotiating Committee (SJNC); resulting in national agreements on the terms and conditions of employment of teachers, the career structure and allocation of promoted posts within each school (laid out according to a clear formula related to school roll) and even the job descriptions of teachers at each level in the school system. Disputes and ongoing issues within the broad national framework were to be resolved locally by joint meetings of directors of children's services (the paid officials responsible, among other things, for the organisation and support of schools within a local authority), councillors and teacher representatives ('Joint Consultative Committees' – JCC). Under the terms of the new agreement ('A Teaching Profession for the 21st Century' (SEED, 2001a)), some scope for local flexibility in these negotiations, albeit tightly monitored, was allowed within a new national negotiation structure, the SNCT (Scottish Negotiating Committee for Teachers).

These national negotiations defined the professional hierarchy in Scottish teaching: class teacher, principal teacher, depute headteacher and headteacher. In addition, the new position of 'Chartered Teacher', created through the 2001 national agreement (SEED, 2001a), rewards class teacher expertise and cannot be assigned any formal leadership or management duties. The General Teaching Council of Scotland (GTCS) (see online) has meantime continued to develop its role in regulating the profession.

Standards of performance for schools are also prescribed nationally through the work of Her Majesty's Inspectors of Education (HMIE). This public body inspects schools, local education authorities and other agencies providing education, identifies and shares good practice, and produces widely used descriptions of different 'levels' of practice in key areas of the work of schools. Their descriptors of weak and very good practice in schools (HMIE, 2007a) are widely used in school self-evaluation within the Scottish system and have attracted considerable interest in other educational systems.

Hitherto this strong national framing, involving highly specified functions for each post, clearly defined job descriptions and the resolution of any disputes through local authority JCCs in which staff association representatives saw their job as to 'hold lines' set nationally, has restricted local decision-making at school level. Moreover, beyond the organisation structure, the increasing expectation in school inspections of compliance with a national curriculum, with nationally specified ways of managing school processes and with national recommendations on teaching and learning approaches increased the pressures to uniformity and conformity with a 'national best practice model'. Additionally, Scottish schools remain part of the services offered by multi-purpose local authorities, who retain control over all aspects of educational policy, although generally local authorities accepting substantial policy leadership from national sources. The corporate local authority influence, felt for example in matters such as budgetary processes, or complex arrangements for securing building maintenance funds, often work against the grain with community-based schools, fitting better with the kinds of services which are directly managed from the local authority HQ, such as cleansing or planning. The introduction of increasingly rationalised bureaucratic structures within Scottish local government in the 1980s, with headteachers reporting to area officers or assistant directors within hierarchical bureaucratic structures of local government, also tended to emphasise the 'branch outlet' image of the local school. Class teachers might face some six or seven layers of hierarchy within the school before getting to a level where an education authority official might accept final responsibility for a decision, or be willing to consider matters of policy. Within this strong national and local bureaucratic framing, this role of the headteacher as 'local branch manager' was strongly underlined, although not always articulated. For many headteachers, the experience of recent political changes was of increasing accountability for decisions matched with reducing decision-making responsibility.

Significantly, the model of resolution of conflicts of interest which might arise was essentially political (through the local JCC), and the teachers' professional association, the GTCS, also operated on a political model, being controlled by teachers elected on a union 'slate'. Professional independence was not so much about the devolution of responsibility for decision-making, and the associated accountability, to the level of professional practice but was more typically characterised as being exercised through industrial dispute and resolution between employer and employee. Teachers in this model accepted that many of the key professional decisions in their work (curriculum, assessment models, working practices within school) would be made elsewhere, since, as a trade off, they retained control of where and how they spent a substantial proportion of the working week. The tendency for the professional to be constructed as the political can be seen in relation to some key educational policy debates of this era – in relation, for example, to the development of the Higher Still programme of curricular and examination reform at age16+. Teachers could only resist what they saw as the impractical and potentially damaging aspects of the reform through their use of union muscle (Paterson, 2000b).

Schools in Scotland, as part of the public education service, could in summary be characterised as 'branch outlets' of a national system, with limited flexibility applied at local authority level, and restricted responsibility at the level of the school, where the headteacher largely operating as a local branch manager, required to demonstrate compliance with a set of arrangements and agreements decided elsewhere. Although some recent policy changes, such as the 'Curriculum for Excellence', which offers more challenges than solutions, have the potential to open this model up, there remains a high degree of regulation from outside the school.

Yet alongside this hierarchical bureaucratic model of school organisation, with its clear lines of reporting, its nationally prescribed roles and structures, and its political process for the resolution of conflicts, sits a very different model of school organisation. This is clear if we start not from the viewpoint of those who share in the organisation and decision-making associated with schooling as a national public service, but from the experience of those who live and work within schools for at least 190 working days annually. The tension between these two viewpoints runs through every aspect of school analysis and is a feature of much international literature on schools and schooling (Barber, 1994; Ranson, 1994; Ungoed-Thomas, 1997; Sergiovanni, 1994; Riley 1998b). In this alternative model, schools can equally successfully be characterised as organic organisations, as living complex communities of practice in which many unpredictable, and unplanned, lines of power and influence cross over the nicely drawn lines of the bureaucratic structure.

In schools families may be in receipt of the 'service' for 4, 10 or even 18 years or more (depending on sibling gaps) and will participate in a range of relationships with the school which go beyond functional service and exhibit many of the characteristics of contemporary community. Key stakeholders are not only recipients of the service as a transaction, but closely involved in its successful delivery. Indeed their active participation in the service is a necessary part of its delivery, particularly in the case of school pupils who as 'learners' at the least acquiesce and at best are actively involved in the process of their own learning, which cannot take place without them. This contribution made by pupils and parents to the overall ethos of the school as an organisation cannot be specified nationally and varies greatly from school to school. In this model of schools as organisations, the bureaucratic specification might be seen as a skeleton, on which local communities build the 'real school'.

Another 'organic' aspect of schools as organisations derives from their aims. Although some aims of the public education system are externally defined, once a school community has been created it has the capacity to develop a concept of itself as a community and to derive a set of aims internal to that community. Indeed independently of the community (or external) definition of aims, each individual may identify educational aims internal to himself or herself. The aims schools set for themselves, and which others to whom they are accountable have also set for them, are often to do with self-esteem, development of the whole child, engendering respect for all, treating all equally – aims which require non-hierarchical relationships of mutual trust and respect. A number of features of the development of Scottish schools mark the move from hierarchical bureaucracy (in which the pupil might be characterised as the worker at the bottom of the hierarchy, with limited control over his or her work) to empowering community: the abandonment of corporal punishment and the progressive introduction of more rational, then educative, disciplinary processes; the development in practice then as a bureaucratised requirement in the Standards in Scotland's Schools Etc Act 2000 (SEED, 2000a)) of pupil and parent involvement in school decision-making; the change in emphasis in 'target-setting' (a government initiative of the late 1990s) from top–down expectation, to a process of negotiation with individual learners to assist them in planning their learning.

Schools are enormously 'over organised' places, with all kinds of national and local prescription regulating a great deal of their activity. Equally schools are enormously unpredictable places with all kinds of local influences to do with the people who are in them, who bring different things in the door each day, and some of whom at least are none too impressed with the role in which they are cast by national, local or even school requirements. This comparison of organic/community and mechanical/bureaucratic systems as applied to schools is not intended to offer a comprehensive organisational analysis, but to provide illustrations of the complexity of their organisational characteristics, of the interplay of many of the contextual factors which affect the decision-making of teachers and headteachers and of the dangers of adopting too simplistic a framework in trying to describe or prescribe the real or desirable activities of schools.

Further complexity is added by the non-hierarchical networks within which school staff and stakeholders participate – networks and alliances (formal and informal) across schools and the wider educational community and within local communities – subject associations, teacher associations, headteacher associations, local authority quality assurance officers, partnership work with other public agencies, such as the police, and voluntary sector organisations … and many beyond these contribute to the richness and complexity of an individual school mix. The resulting lines of force and influence, and the consequent complexity of participation in leadership activities within the school, mess up the tidy organisational map of bureaucracy and introduce a welcome human tension into the framing and experience of schooling.

The importance of the cultural mix which results from these complex interplays in shaping the experience of individuals within an organisational community is widely accepted (Schein, 1985). In contemporary plural school communities, culture is complex. There may well be an official culture ('the way we do things around here') which is designed to fit with the aims: a set of rituals and displays. However this may itself be riven with paradox, as some of the values that the school community holds may not fit well together; comprehensive schools value each child equally but many place a high value publicly (through 'Roll of Honour' boards in the school entrance hall for example) on the highest academic achiever each year. These confused mixed messages from the intermingling of different traditions and expectations can and do co-exist. There are also innumerable rich subcultures of enormous importance to the individuals in the school (e.g. the subculture associated with a particular weekly football game may be the only bit of the school week where particular pupils feel at home).

There is an extensive literature, on the cultures (and subcultures) of schools as organisations. Ball (1987) and Hamilton (2002) illustrate the tensions within school subcultures and how this impacts on the individuals within the school. Recently considerable attention has been given, in the research and practice literature used to support teachers' professional development, to the growth of schools' capacity to improve and develop (Hopkins *et al.*, 1997; Stoll, 1999; Harris, 2002). A defining organisational image of the improving school now widely used and adapted from business models, in the context of helping schools to become better at their core mission of providing a good education for their pupils, is of the school as a 'learning organisation', an 'intelligent school' (MacGilchrist *et al.*, 2004). This dynamic, self-aware model of schooling offers an image of a community in which both teachers and learners are aware of what makes for successful learning. They give primacy to developing their capacity to change and respond, respect the diversity of learning and work with and for each other to develop a healthy climate of mutual support and respect. This image commands widespread support. It recognises that schools are not organisations to be judged by their external effectiveness – their ability to produce products such as cars, televisions, computers or services such as audit or consultancy advice. Many of the worthwhile outcomes of schooling are internal to the school community, and indeed internal to the individuals within that community – outcomes such as a love of learning, and a capacity to live with and work with others. In the learning community, leadership is widely distributed among the different individuals, as each takes responsibility for his or her own participation and for his or her own learning. The 'Curriculum for Excellence' *aims* to capture this dynamic open-ended character of the best schooling but sits in tension with the politically derived Scottish state school model – in which political struggles at national level between teacher associations, government ministers and officials (including HMIE) and local government officers, and the resulting compromises of policy, defined the school as essentially the 'implementation site' of national initiatives, with only political agreements on teachers' contracts offering some protection in limiting the pace and scale of centrally prescribed change. Leadership, in this model, could be seen as essentially about power. Far removed from the rationale and detail of national educational initiatives, teachers often experienced this power through 'top–down' impositions, evident most clearly in the often poorly worked out practical details of implementation, details which rendered irrelevant the value-based rationale for change. This experience of the last twenty years of imposed change has engendered a healthy disrespect for change in many staff rooms. The school which appears to emerge from the story is one in which much of what defines its character, its relationships and its capacity – the curriculum it teaches, the qualifications and conditions of service of its staff, its structures and systems – is decided somewhere else. The job of those locally has been to take whatever that decision was, however poor its design, and to make it work.

Yet despite this image of recent change, despite the often unappealing political character of national developments, and despite the fact that the learning was often painful and could perhaps have been more evenly planned and developed, many Scottish schools clearly can be characterised as 'learning organisations'. This can be seen most clearly in public information that gets under the surface of the organisational descriptions characteristic of Inspection reports (HM Inspectors of Schools) such as the reports published by the Scottish School Ethos Network (see online).

As organisations, schools in Scotland then exhibit and are defined both by very clear and tight mechanical, bureaucratic, rational characteristics and also by a range of organic, holistic, unpredictable characteristics. The tension between these two has driven the story of school development, sometimes through politics, sometimes through professional practice, into the present day. A key turning point recently was the 'Higher Still' fiasco (in which teachers delivered on the effective teaching of a new certification system at 16+, but the national system failed to cope with the complexity of assessment it had itself prescribed)

The new Scottish Parliament and Scottish ministers both recognised that the state education system, even in a country as small as Scotland, could not be centrally planned in detail (Paterson, 2000b). A deeper political understanding of the complexity of development is also expressed in the Standards in Scotland's Schools Etc Act (SEED, 2000a) with its recognition of the importance of both national and local determination. This Act has both a strong 'top–down' and 'bottom–up' character. Firstly, it requires all local authorities to draw up improvement plans to demonstrate how they intend to ensure that their schools continue to improve their performance in relation to specified national priorities for the public education system. Schools must also plan, in the context of their local authority improvement plan, how they intend to improve. This appears a very centralised, and bureaucratic, system for ensuring that all local authorities and all schools fit into the national system of priorities. However, within the same Act, schools are required to consult about priorities for development with their key stakeholders – staff, pupils and parents. This offers the prospect of more 'bottom–up' empowerment than has been typical of Scottish schools in the past. Genuine consultation and involvement might throw up different sets of priorities, different ways of interpreting what 'school improvement' means. It is no coincidence that those same tensions which we have broadly characterised in this chapter as arising from conflict between competing forces (the 'outside in' and the 'inside out') are so readily seen at the heart of this important piece of legislation, which frames the way in which Scottish schools will develop in the future. The Act encapsulates the dynamic plurality of leadership within school communities.

These outside in and inside out forces can then be set in a context of the competing values at play in schooling, and competing visions of school purpose. The National Debate of 2002/3 in Scotland (SEED, 2003a) established a wide degree of support for the five broad national priorities established for the Scottish education system: 'attainment and achievement', 'framework for learning', 'inclusion and equality', 'values and citizenship' and 'learning for life'. The 'Curriculum for Excellence', whatever else it will be, is clearly not a rigidly organised curriculum to be delivered in all schools. Never, it seems, has there been a greater need for highly skilled education professionals to lead education forward in local school communities. Indeed, 'leadership', particularly the leadership of the headteacher, is now often seen as the key 'solution', the place where the tensions and competing forces come together and are made to work together positively:

> Headteachers lead in the creation of a shared strategic vision and aim for the school, which inspire and motivate children and young people, staff and all members of the school community and its partners and sets high standards for every learner. (SEED, 2005c)

The recent HMIE report 'Leadership for learning: the challenges of leading in a time of change' (HMIE, 2007b) outlines clearly these high expectations of headteachers. But what is leadership, who is involved in it and what are the experiences of those in these challenging leadership roles? The next two chapters explore these issues in greater detail.

CHAPTER 2

LEADERSHIP, SCHOOL LEADERSHIP AND HEADSHIP

Are schools bureaucratically ordered institutions of the state, accountable to technocratic experts appointed by elected politicians for the efficient delivery of politically determined objectives or are they moral communities, making social capital through relationships and local discussion, or are they both of these at the same time? The previous chapter established the context within which public schools operate, looking at the 'school' part of school leadership. This chapter will consider the 'leadership' part, providing a conceptual context within which to consider who are the leaders and what leadership role should they be playing, by considering leadership theory in general, reflecting on the differences between leadership and management, analysing levels and types of leadership in schools and reflecting on the particular role of the headteacher.

Leadership theories

There are clear stages in the evolution of leadership theory are. Historically, the perception was that leaders were born not made. Initial research on leadership centred on figures who had made their mark on events – the generals and monarchs or influential 'great men' view first promoted by Thomas Carlyle (1841). Subsequent research inspired by this notion focuses on *traits* or personality characteristics discernible in such people. There have been attempts to identify that core of traits or common characteristics and qualities and subsequently behaviours unique to great leaders. The military for many years were concerned with identifying key characteristics and training their leaders appropriately. This tradition reflects the belief that what a leader does is important and that the skills of leadership can be learned and developed.

Howard Gardner (1995) reviewed successful leadership with an interesting perspective of 'leading minds' of the twentieth century whose thoughts and actions have inspired a range of followers. Gardner suggests that such diverse characters as Churchill and Einstein mark the 'two ends of a continuum that denotes the capacity of a person (or a group of persons) to influence other people', and poses the question of his choice of other leaders 'Who ultimately had the greater influence?' The choice of leaders for his discussion reflects his consideration of *direct* and *indirect* leadership (in Gardner's terms, Churchill was a *direct* leader while Einstein represents *indirect* leadership). *Ordinary* leaders who are effective but have nothing essentially new to say are contrasted with *innovative* leaders who bring new perspectives and ultimately with *visionary* leaders who, he suggests, are a rare breed. He categorises Gandhi and Jean Monnet as two such visionaries.

Forms of leadership and their importance for schools

Concepts of leadership and ideas about leadership in general are comprehensively documented (Schein, 1985; Leithwood *et al.*, 2000). A list of different forms of leadership derived from this tradition might include:

- authoritarian
- charismatic
- collaborative
- contingent
- cultural
- ethical
- moral
- participative
- servant
- situational
- transactional
- transformational
- visionary.

This listing provides a sample of some of the descriptors of leadership. Some, for example authoritarian, charismatic and collaborative may be seen as self-explanatory. Others, at first sight, a little less so. What forms are regarded as particularly effective in schools? Are there other approaches to leadership that might apply in schools, for example instructional leadership or curriculum leadership?

Some forms of leadership may be about *style*. Morrison (2002, pp.77–82) identifies the importance of the work of Goleman (2000) on emotional intelligence to depict six styles of leadership and Fullan's use of each (2001, pp. 41–2) (Figure 2.1):

There are so many leadership theories that inevitably some, while interesting from an academic perspective, may offer less to school leaders than others. Even within the narrow field of education, leadership studies are now so diverse and wide ranging as to require a map (Ribbins and Gunter, 2002) requiring more than a little interpretative skill on the part of the reader. The most extensive recent discussion of the wide variety of educational leadership studies can be found in Gunter (2001) who provides

Figure 2.1: Styles of leadership

Affiliative	*Authoritative*	*Coaching*
• Creates harmony and strong interpersonal relationships in an organisation • Putting people first • Helpful in overcoming fear of change	• Gets people working to achieve the vision • May not be good listeners	• Develops colleagues for the long-term future • Helpful in overcoming fear of change
Coercive	*Democratic*	*Pacesetting*
• 'Do as I say' approach • Poor listening skills?	• 'Let's talk about how we progress' • Over listening skills?	• Expects self-direction and high-quality performance from colleagues • Poor listening skills?

a comprehensive guide to recent theories and critique. Southworth (1998, pp. 36–55) in his more school-focused discussion of leadership theories, justifies a more limited 'set' of leadership types:

- *Situational leadership*, where the leader uses sensitive situational knowledge to guide decision-making;
- *Instrumental and expressive leadership*, in which the leader combines a strong task focus with a commitment to achieving the task with and through people;
- *Cultural leadership* is concerned with values and beliefs, attitudes, understandings and symbols and rituals. Cultural leaders are aware of these and often set norms for an organisation often by modelling or 'walking the talk'. In the study which the Hay Group undertook into the leadership abilities of a sample of headteachers and business leaders (Hay McBer, 2000), the strongest leadership effect within an organisation is on the organisational climate, which in turn effects the performance of all those within the organisation.
- *Transactional leadership* is leadership redefined as skill in bargaining and exchange – in this model, skilful trading of interests allows the organisation to function effectively.
- *Transformational leadership* is about getting behind the actions. If the values and motivations of those who follow can be changed or developed, then a much deeper level of commitment, able to cope with new and changing situations, will emerge. Recently this form of leadership has been caricatured (Gunter, 2001, pp. 68–75) as simply the use of more subtle and sometimes devious

devices to achieve leadership purposes, consigning 'followers' to a passive role.

This critique is a reminder that, although it may be tempting for those who read leadership books (who tend to be those who aspire to leadership positions) to invest 'heroic' qualities, or transformational powers, in the leader, the kinds of leadership which might apply to plural democratic organisations will be more complex. Recent writing on this theme, including the analysis of leadership by HMIE (HMIE, 2007b, pp. 11–29) has often made use of the concept of 'distributed leadership'.

Distributed leadership

The National College for School Leadership (Bennett *et al.*, 2003, p. 3) commissioned a study designed to investigate the extent to which:

- there was a common understanding of the term;
- writing in the field covered both formal and informal leadership;
- the literature provided practical advice to heads and other school leaders in developing distributed leadership within their organisations.

The study found disparate definitions of the concept of distributed leadership which has a variety of meanings. In Gunter's critique (2001), leadership studies have often conflated leadership with leaders, and in educational terms defined leaders according to position in the schools. Many such studies have therefore focused on the headteacher, to the exclusion of all other leadership activities in the school. Gronn (2000, p. 232) provides a theoretical academic structure to support the common-sense observation that:

> distributed leadership is even manifest in what appear to be the most self-evident and uncontestable instances of stand-alone … leadership. In the case of … dictatorships . . . in which a military general takes charge. While the individuals may exercise … supreme … power, they generally act on behalf of or with or with the blessing of an army council, a junta … on which they are also heavily dependent … in more familiar democratic arrangements, there are often vast networks of specialist advisers, minders and officials … In each of these instances, the division of leadership labour … can be demonstrated to be shared and dispersed …

In this view, leadership studies which have focused excessively on the individual are limited in their ability to interpret and understand what really is going on because they are conceptually flawed, considering only one aspect of the agency and activity of the school. Taking this view, a broader vision of leadership in schools emerges, well beyond a narrow focus on the headteacher as 'visionary champion' (Gronn, 2000).

Gronn is not so much writing of delegation of powers to colleagues, or of senior management teams but rather of different ways of working together in a complex human system where the dynamics of relationships in a work setting are interdependent, intricate and long term (Gronn, 2003). He argues that in reality many people in school exercise leadership, including unpromoted teachers (teacher leaders) and students and that stand-alone leadership simply does not (and cannot) exist in schools. He distinguishes several levels of interaction and joint action:

- spontaneous collaboration arising from common interest and concerns;
- 'intuitive working relations' where over a period of time working relationships develop to the point where interactions between familiar partners become smooth and collaborative. The basis of development and progress thus becomes effective collaborations rooted in mutually rewarding working relationships;
- through formally constituted groupings of staff which may be short-term working groups or longer-term collegial structures. He suggests these working partnerships may operate face to face and collectively or people may work separately towards a shared goal, with the task being led and managed with at least the consent and often the active participation of those involved.

Morrison (2002) applies complexity theory to school leadership. In doing so he posits that unpredictability is inherent and that the operation of complex systems (like schools) cannot be understood by analysing parts of the whole in isolation. Taking a true systems perspective, he holds that the elements of the system and the interactions or flows between those elements are key to the effectiveness of the organisation. He proposes a dynamic vision of leadership, arguing that long-term planning is pointless because change is continuous and that organisations that focus on stability will fail. In addition, he suggests that leaders do not have the power to determine how things work in a context of multiple opposing forces, that their power is limited and that they can only work with and through others to achieve progress. Complexity theory is rooted in an assumption that change and unpredictability are normal.

Like Gronn, Morrison suggests that a focus on a formal leader is insufficient. His application of complexity theory offers a further insight: a developmental framework of leadership, where he argues that a developmental path may be conceptualised with 'command and control' top–down leadership as an early and immature form of leadership, built on assumptions of stability and the feasibility of effective control. This leads to line management with delegation and clear and certain lines of accountability. But these, he says, are insufficient to cope with a rapidly changing environment and the narrowness of power, in disempowering others, gives way to a more developed form of leadership in team working: the active development and nurturing of teams. The next stage, according to Morrison, is distributed leadership, with all that it promises in terms of participation. The final stage concludes with current thinking on servant leadership, where the role of the leader is not to direct but to work with and for others to achieve common goals in a changing environment. This progressive model reflects the development of selected thinking on leadership, but he proposes that it also describes the development of leadership in practice over time (and across rather than within individual leaders), suggesting that servant leadership is the most complex and mature form. This has some face validity in a rapidly changing environment. Logically, steps beyond servant leadership are possible but are not proposed in his current model.

Concerns over servant leadership have been voiced, however, in relation to exclusivity and the favouring of the group or organisation's objectives and preferences over wider concerns. The intentions of servant leadership may be no more attainable in practice than the mythical control of martinets at the other end of the developmental spectrum he proposes. However, his approach makes a valuable contribution in its critical analysis of control-focused bureaucratic management, reminding us of the costs of fixed job descriptions and rigid procedures, policy mountains and long-term planning in a changing environment. There is an implication here also of the relative fruitlessness of laboured accountability against the past rather than a focus on the present and future.

Leadership in Scottish schools

Scottish society experiences the aspects of contemporary democracy which Gronn cites above. Scots, moreover, are often highly suspicious of leaders who seek to exercise excessive power. An emphasis on consumer choice and individuality is paralleled by a suspicion of over-regimentation and institutional practices based solely on authority. There is an expectation that social practices to which individuals are asked to conform should be based on a (usually utilitarian) rationale which can be scrutinised by those affected and which makes sense to them. The civic community accepts considerable diversity in lifestyle, personal preference and culturally framed behaviour. A broad range of freedoms of behaviour and expression are balanced by a commitment to processes of debate and consensus building; the acquisition of power to make decisions takes place through a political process of persuasion in which almost all adults have a restricted voice, through their vote and their ability to speak freely. While sometimes seen more in action and reaction than in precise prose, these values are grounded in a widespread commitment to the notion of human rights. The political power of the state to limit, direct and constrain the behaviour of citizens is balanced by a series of protections, which nurture and support individual freedoms.

This widespread acceptance, and legislative enactment, of a substantial range of human rights, sees these as inviolable, offering significant protections to individuals in their dealings with social institutions. Young people share in these rights. The Children's (Scotland) Act of 1995 spells out what this means in specific situations in which young people may find themselves (Chakrabarti and Cadman, 2003). This democratic model of community participation and formation, in which individuals are aware in broad terms of a balance between social needs and individual rights, underpins the ethos and values of the Scottish school. Both at primary and secondary level, important social values – loosely defined if at all, but fulfilling a 'mythic' function – are accepted and internalised within school communities.

In recent years, the more passive notion of 'equality of opportunity' (with its implication that individuals will vary in the extent to which they take advantage of that opportunity) has been replaced within the Scottish civic consensus with a broader and more active notion of 'social inclusion', a term which has been widely accepted politically. In this view, it is part of the function of public policy, and public institutions such as schools, to promote actively the interests and involvement of all individuals. No one should be 'selected out'. Within the student body in Scottish state schools, a tolerance of difference runs alongside a sense of justice and fairness (Carr and Landon, 1998; 1999). Increasingly, the quality of schooling is seen to depend on the character of the relationships formed within the school. Schools and their teaching staff aim to develop trust, a sense of common purpose and a widely supported rationale for existing or new patterns of institutional practice and behaviour which makes sense in terms of the interests of the young people (Murray, 2002).

These characteristics of Scottish society, of the political and legislative framework which defines its behavioural rules, and of Scottish schools, ensure that power, and associated leadership responsibilities, are widely distributed within most of our schools. This pattern accords with Gronn's (2000) model of distributed leadership and raises issues of collaboration between staff in schools. Leadership is exercised through the significant actions of a large number of individuals and groups that have an impact on the character of a school community. These include national and local political leaders (and the officials who serve them), who frame educational policy and determine resourcing, professional staff within and external to schools, parents and carers in each community and the pupils of a given school. Each of these groups, and the significant leadership role which they play, will now be considered in turn.

National political leadership

Political leadership in relation to schools is exercised nationally in Scotland through the Scottish Government (see online) (termed Scottish Executive prior to 2007), its ministers and supporting civil servants and agencies and the committees of the new Scottish Parliament (see online).

In the twenty years after 1980, as we have discussed in Chapter 1, Scotland developed a very centralised school system. This was characterised by Scottish Office direction, Inspectorate leadership of policy, an absence of educational leadership at education authority level (where year-on-year budget cuts and political defensiveness against what was seen as a hostile UK government limited scope for creativity) and an inspection regime which expected compliance rather than effectiveness. Little headroom was allowed for local leadership politically, professionally or within school communities. A range of centrally directed initiatives – Standard Grade certification for those aged 14–16, the Technical and Vocational Education Initiative, '5–14' (Scotland's fudged version of a centrally mandated national curriculum for this age group, which allowed for local discretion both in some aspects of curriculum and in the pacing of implementation), Staff Appraisal, the Main Committee's (SOED, 1986) deal on teachers' pay and conditions and 'Higher Still', a new scheme of post-16 national examinations – regularised the Scottish system, reducing diversity and local creativity. For some, school leadership was construed as technical management, whose function was to implement solutions devised elsewhere and whose success would be assessed by measures of efficiency and effectiveness in service delivery. Professional debate in Scotland often focused on how best to deliver the nationally planned agenda. Centralisation of policy however does not mean effective implementation. Many of these centralising policies were only partially or ineffectively implemented. The best documented example is the Higher Still debacle (Paterson, 2000b) which finally discredited the view that there was only room for one level of leadership in the national education system.

The Education Minister who gave a decisive response to this situation was Jack McConnell, a former teacher whose direct access to 'field professionals' provided him with alternative sources of advice to that received from Inspectors and civil servants. In a series of highly publicised visits to schools early in his tenure (see, for example, Scottish Executive, 2001), he made it clear that the power of school leadership would shift from the centre and be distributed more to schools. After becoming First Minister (McConnell, 2002), he endorsed and reinforced this shift by his decision to remove the Inspectorate altogether from a policy advice role. This had an immediate effect on the tone and character of school inspections. Inspectors were now said to be prepared to engage with the agenda set locally within a school community rather than inspect schools for the performance in relation to a national policy template. Inspections were to become 'outcome based' and were no longer to be driven by compliance, though this change has been more apparent than real, since the most reliable outcome-based measures are national examination statistics. This move was the most dramatic evidence of a change of culture, and shift in power, in the leadership of educational policy and schools in Scotland, but there had already been signs in Scottish Executive policy of a willingness to disperse power and encourage local decision-making and creativity, even if this was held in tension with the desire to control and shape change, as highlighted in the description in Chapter 1 of the Standards in Scotland's Schools etc Act (SEED, 2000a). Scottish Executive Education Dept Circular 3/2001 (SEED, 2001b) freed up the 'managed' school curriculum, by encouraging schools to make local decisions in relation to individual needs rather than pushing all pupils through the previous curriculum model in which time was rigidly allocated to modes of study at age 14–16, and to curriculum areas, 5–14. This broader, more complex, vision of curriculum has been carried through into consultation, underway at the time of publication, on a new model for Scottish curriculum planning, *Building the Curriculum* (see SEED, 2008).

Some studies (Murphy *et al.*, 2002a; 2002b) show that the capacity of education authorities, and schools, to respond to national strategy varies greatly, increasing the potential for inequality in provision. Moreover, the previous Scottish Executive made significant changes to the arrangements for involving parents in school-level decision-making (SEED, 2006a). This new legislation saw the abolition of School Boards, and their replacement by 'Parent Councils', designed to be less formal and more inclusive in their character. It is too early to assess the impact of these changes. Nonetheless, significant changes in climate and structure have taken place. National political strategy has encouraged greater community participation in the business of schooling, while setting out some challenging broad aims through the definition of five national priorities and the 'Curriculum for Excellence'. At the time of writing, it is unclear if there will be any significant political shifts consequent on the election of a new administration in Scotland in 2007, however it seems unlikely that there will be any reduction in the importance accorded to leadership and leadership development, given the demographic need to train and recruit many new headteachers in the decade ahead (HMIE, 2007b, p. 11).

Leadership within education authorities

Although much of the focus of research and policy discussion is on national government, within the Scottish system, schools are owned, operated and supported in their work by education authorities. A full discussion of the legal position and functioning of these authorities can be found in Green (1999) and Bloomer (2003). Within the limits imposed by the national and centralising forces outlined above, and those imposed by corporate strategies within local government, significant variations can be found across Scotland's local authorities in the quality, range and creativity of school provision and support. Some of this variation is now evident in the Inspection reports which are being published into the quality of the work (HMIE, 2008a) of local authorities. Frequent stories in the Scottish educational press, together with 8-page supplements on particular authorities (e.g. Renfrew Council, 2002), provide anecdotal and uncritical description of initiative and development at local level. This leadership work of local authorities is under-researched and often remains hidden from objective scrutiny. The interest of the local press is more likely to be stirred by news of 're-zoning' schools or problems with new buildings, rather than complex educational or curricular policies, or unusual and creative systems for supporting and developing staff. This does not mean, however, that the creative leadership role of local authorities in the Scottish context should be underplayed. National government (the SEED) makes it clear that responsibility for implementation and delivery rests at local level, while the 2000 Act requires all local authorities to prepare local improvement plans, outlining how they intend to continue to deliver a better educational service to their communities. The recent OECD report (OECD, 2008, pp. 34–7) provides a strong endorsement of both the role and capacity of local authorities to continue to manage school-based education, while recognising that local authorities vary greatly in the extent to which they use their potential power to seek and create local solutions.

Local authorities can also have a significant impact on the character of the school communities which they fund and maintain. If they adopt bureaucratic and hierarchical approaches to managing their schools, they can inhibit local creativity, recreating at local level the atmosphere of inhibited professional compliance which was until recently in Scotland the prerogative of the Inspectorate. Initiatives which SEED may have intended to be interpreted flexibly at school level might be framed as directives at local authority level, restoring the school to the role of 'branch outlet' so recently abandoned by national government. Interpersonal relationships between headteachers, quality improvement officers, heads of service and directors of children's services can all impact significantly on teamwork and partnership. The potential tension in leadership between the local authority and the headteacher can be seen in the mixed responses of headteachers in a recent survey of headteachers and depute headteachers in Scottish secondary schools (Murphy, 2003a; 2003b; 2003c). Some 48 per cent either agreed or strongly agreed with the statement 'My local authority doesn't add value, it takes it away by introducing an unnecessary layer of bureaucracy.'

Local authorities are further challenged to improve the teamwork across different professional services for children, particularly children at risk. The recent Scottish Executive work on 'Getting It Right for Every Child' (SEED, 2006b) demonstrates clearly the challenges of ensuring that services to support young people are 'joined up' across professional boundaries and competing bureaucracies. The leadership role of local authorities is clearly an intensely important part of the mix in the Scottish school system.

Parental and pupil leadership within school communities

Lindsay Paterson's research (2002) into the role of parents in supporting their children's learning and achievements gained wide publicity in the Scottish press. Based on statistical analysis of school leaver data, he suggested that the children of middle-class families in state comprehensive schools performed within the same range of results as the children of middle-class families at independent schools. The conclusion that parental background has a substantial impact on educational achievement is widely reported beyond Scotland. This involvement of parents in promoting and supporting a certain model of learning, in which social conformity within school is rewarded by progressive access to credentials and the opportunities beyond school to which they give access, can dominate a school's educational agenda. Parents, albeit often in passive and supportive roles, participate in leading school communities in certain directions. It is not, of course, only middle-class parents who can or do play leadership roles. The case studies cited by Murray (2002) involve parents and carers within widely differing school communities in taking responsibility for shared leadership.

School Boards in Scotland also played a major leadership role in some school communities, providing the local catalyst for political pressure in relation to the standard of buildings, or acting as a parental voice in relation to a headteacher who is felt to ignore the wider school community. It is too early to assess whether Parent Councils will play a similarly strong role.

Recently there have also been signs of increasing pupil leadership within Scottish schools. This can be seen, for example, in the widespread adoption of 'circle time' approaches in primary schools; in inclusive approaches to bullying and to other pastoral and curricular concerns (playground 'buddies' are now found in many Scottish schools, 'reading supporters' in many others); student consultation, at school and at local authority level, is another developing feature of student participation in leadership. (HMIE, 2007a, pp. 21–2).

Even at national level, students are playing an increasingly important role in policy debate seen, for example, in the role that students played, through the media and through evidence to the parliamentary committees, in shaping policy reaction to the Higher Still debacle (Paterson, 2000b).

Just as among staff, where the 'pecking order' of the staff room may not match the hierarchies of those in positions of seniority, student leadership in schools can also take different forms. For example, the unofficial leadership of the drug dealer among those adolescents who seek risks can be every bit as important in determining student behaviours within a particular peer group as any official leadership roles played out in class or in school.

Staff leadership within school communities

Staff play substantial leadership roles within school communities. The range of such leadership is considerable and includes peer leadership within staff rooms and key work groups, for example in involving staff in community events beyond the classroom such as seasonal school shows, or charity fundraising. There is curricular and instructional leadership from effective teachers and community leadership from office and reception staff who set a bright, responsive and inclusive tone for the school. There is leadership from school caretakers who take a pride in putting safety first, and who in a hundred and one small exchanges with students and staff throughout a week maintain a profile for safe movement and risk awareness in a school building. Few of these illustrative instances of leadership derive from hierarchically ordered positions of power or influence. Of course these promoted positions, such as headteacher, depute headteacher or principal teacher also offer many opportunities for leadership within the school community, and often carry an expectation of leadership in important areas of school life. In a striking recent illustration of these changes in contemporary thinking about 'leadership', the Headteachers Association of Scotland has changed its name to 'School Leaders Scotland', adopting an inclusive approach to membership based on the concept of 'leadership', not the role of headteacher itself.

The headteacher

These instances of leadership outwith and within school communities – leadership which orders, which influences and which makes a difference to others – offer an insight into the complexity of leadership activity, and the wide range of those who participate in leadership within our schools. However within the Scottish system, the headteacher has played, and is expected to continue to play, a key role in balancing out the different forces at work and in setting a direction with and for the school community within the guidance offered locally and nationally and for the remainder of this study of school leadership it is therefore the headteacher who will be our primary concern. The influence exercised through the behaviours of the headteacher has been widely acknowledged in a range of studies as being of particular importance (Leithwood *et al.*, 1999; Day *et al.*, 2000; Tomlinson *et al.*, 1999; MacBeath, 1998). Scottish HMIE, as others elsewhere (DES, 1977) have consistently cited the central importance and accountability of the leadership role of the headteacher in assisting school communities to realise their aims and ambitions. The good practices which they wish to see developed in all schools are summarised in their recent publication 'Leadership for learning: the challenges of leading in a time of change' (HMIE, 2007b). Whatever the merits or demerits of the individualist approach to leadership implied by an excessive focus on headteachers who have substantial bureaucratic positional power within schools, there is no doubt that for the headteachers themselves, for those who share in headship (through deputising for example, or through the collegial operation of 'senior teams' (Wallace and Hall, 1994; Wallace and Huckman, 1996) in schools) and for those who are directed in their work by headteachers, the leadership style and behaviours of the headteacher can make a substantial difference to their experience of the school community. Headteachers in Scotland are delegated substantial authority, but operate under the direction of the local authority. Teachers are also directed, albeit within limits agreed nationally, by the headteacher. The use of the word 'direction' in the nationally agreed job descriptions of headteachers and of teachers (SEED, 2001a, Annexe B) emphasises the continuing importance of the bureaucratic model of service delivery in the Scottish state education system. Headteachers in Scotland provide leadership in their school communities within a very tightly externally defined set of roles and limitations on action, in addition to sharing leadership with others within the school community in the ways outlined above.

In the context of this discussion of 'leadership', it is worth noting that neither the now disbanded SJNC nor its replacement the SNCT nor local JCCs have normally involved headteacher representation. As the 'managers' who would require to make any agreements made in these meetings work in practice, it was on the face of it surprising that headteachers should not be so represented, but their presence was often construed as uncomfortable by both the director of education (directors could not be sure if heads would 'toe the party line' in key disputes) and also the teacher associations (who saw headteachers as giving 'management' an extra voice at the negotiations). This practice of excluding headteachers' representatives from key decision-making discussions is a significant contextual factor in limiting the leadership role of the headteacher limits with which Chapter 3 is concerned.

Whatever the limits, there is no doubt that locally in schools, the decisions of headteachers over matters such as timetabling or class allocation can and do have a significant impact on the work experience of teachers and pupils. This capacity for local influence appears to be growing. In the 1980s and 1990s, increasing emphasis was placed through national policy on site-based operational management. This was partly the result in Britain of a politically motivated frustration in the late 1980s with Labour-controlled education authorities (who were seen to be obstacles to change) and a broader professional concern to respond to the lessons on effective provision coming from private sector organisations which had responded well to the challenging economic context of the 1970s and 1980s. It was also, however, an international phenomenon (Caldwell and Spinks, 1995) associated with both the new neo-liberal Right and the professional ambitions of headteachers themselves (Hargreaves and Hopkins, 1991) and new trends in broader management literature (Handy, 1991). The organisations which delivered services effectively and had the capacity to renew themselves in responding to a continually changing world were seen to be those which had a clear mission and purpose but substantial 'shop floor' flexibility in realising that mission within a particular context.

This increasing emphasis on site-based management was one of a number of forces which brought the abilities of the school headteacher into particular focus in national policy. The headteacher in the turbulent political and educational climate of the 1980s and 1990s had to manage change effectively to ensure that a clear path would be found between the 'top–down' policy developments and the 'bottom–up' pressures of expectation on the school system. However, although many sources agreed that the headteacher had never been more important in ensuring the school met its multiple aims, a variety of potentially conflicting models of headship co-existed in the professional, political and bureaucratic spheres, several of which we discuss below.

Headteachers can be seen as the 'local middle manager', acting on behalf of 'head office' and accountable firstly to a line manager within the local authority for the delivery of action in relation to key policies. Famously, perhaps apocryphally, within one Scottish education authority, any questioning by headteachers of the authority's policy would be met by the response 'Look whose name is on your pay cheque … that's whose policy you follow'. Another view might define the headteacher as a key social entrepreneur, able to use a position of power and influence to develop and enhance social capital within communities. In professional literature, headteachers are often conceptualised as the lead learners in communities of learning, modelling and facilitating a new model of lifelong learning. In 'managerialist' models, (Morley and Razool, 1999), the headteacher loses the responsibility for learning and develops a technical role, involving the development and exercise of certain key management and professional skills, which should be learned and practised to ensure competent performance. A different tradition, drawing on thinking about the professions and the ways in which their responsibilities differ from employees whose practice is defined by contractual responsibility, emphasised the moral and professional obligations of headship as a professional practice (Carr, 2000; Sergiovanni, 1994). In a final illustration, drawing from research into the daily experience of headship, the headteacher could be seen as a 'decision-maker', exercising power through many small decisions to keep a school community functioning (Calabrese and Zepeda, 1999).

Undoubtedly, the headteacher does make many decisions, but the complex character of leadership and influence, the framing of public schooling within a broader state and local authority structure and the contested character of schooling and the values which underpin school experience make the context for decision-making very difficult to interpret or generalise – 'Who decides?', 'On what values is the decision based?', 'Whose interests does the decision serve?' – is a constant theme in the story of Scottish, and many other, schools.

A recent English research study illustrating this complexity in the experience of headteachers (Grace, 2002) describes the 'mission conflicts' that are experienced within English Roman Catholic secondary schools and the pressures this has put on the headteachers of these schools. The headteachers are trying both to fulfil what they see as the traditional mission of the Catholic school – an education in faith, moral formation, developing all the talents for effective use and aiming to offer a preferential option for the poor – and yet responding to the pressures of a marketised school system. We lack parallel studies in Scotland, but there is no doubt that real leadership skills and abilities are required in interpreting and responding to the complex and contradictory forces inherent in different competing visions of school purpose, operating from different parts of the broader school systems, or from different parts of the school community itself. Joe Murphy (2002) outlined a new blueprint for school leadership. Murphy views the leader as an *educator* (interpreting the world, including the confused and confusing world of educational policy and purpose) for all those in the school community; as a *community builder* (with all key stakeholders in the school community); and as a *moral steward* (aware of and involved in defining and discussing values). Both Grace and Murphy take the discussion of school headship quite clearly into the realms of leadership practice and a leadership agenda. Yet, clearly, some of the models of headship, some headship practice and some of the roles and functions traditionally carried out by heads may be fairly described as 'management'.

Leadership and management

Schools, we have argued, are both democratic communities with distributed power and a balance between individual and institutional power, and functional bureaucratically ordered institutions designed to deliver a set of outcomes efficiently. Power through position is being eroded in contemporary democracies as hierarchical structures are dismantled or flattened within organisations. Therefore it is within the complex, distributed interaction of leadership and power in decision-making in Scottish schools outlined above that school headteachers, and their close colleagues in management teams, exercise their own leadership.

Allix and Gronn (2005, p. 191) argue that:

> one of the most persistent claims of current leadership orthodoxy, which posits a fundamental distinction between leadership and

management, and leaders and managers ... management is associated with a formal role, as a contextual constraint, whereas leadership is not necessarily so constrained, then it would seem that the concept of management, and of a manager, is one that invites consideration of a situational attribution rather than a dispositional one. In contrast, since leadership is not necessarily, although it can be, associated with a formal organizational role, it would therefore appear to suggest that leadership is a disposition that is attributed to a particular person, rather than an attribution that is based on a particular situation.

Historically there has been an emphasis on management in Scottish schools, but our system is not alone in this. Indeed confusion exists because leadership from powerful positions is so closely related to management practice. Leadership is frequently regarded as an aspect of management. Rost (1998) identifies a range of authors who have attempted to confirm a distinction between management and leadership in organisations: for example, Selznick (1957, p. 24) first suggested that the difference between 'routine' and 'critical' decision-making differentiates leadership from management; Graham (1988, p. 74) concluded that 'Appropriate labels for the person giving orders, monitoring compliance, and administering performance contingency rewards and punishments' included the terms 'supervisor' and 'manager' but does not involve the term 'leader', and Bennis and Nanus (1985, p. 21), when confirming that leading does not mean managing, advised:

> There is a profound difference between management and leadership, and both are important. 'To manage' means 'to bring about, to accomplish, to have change of or responsibility for, to conduct.' 'Leading' is 'influencing, guiding in direction, course, action, opinion.' The distinction is critical. *Managers are people who do things right and leaders are people who do the right thing.* The difference may be summarised as activities of vision and judgement – *effectiveness* versus activities of mastering routines – *efficiency*.

These authors are following in a tradition which Samier (2002, p. 42) derives from Weber, who sees leadership as 'not reducible to a program of training in sequential managerial fads', but as a discipline of valuational orientations. For Weber, educational leadership could offer a counterweight to the managerial efficiencies of busy bureaucracy, which avoids questions of purpose in its pursuit of effectiveness.

Leadership and management in schools

Weber's illustrations were concerned with the university sector, which he felt had a unique role in resisting the domination of the managerialist state. In schools, this message seems to have meaning too. Changes in leadership and management approaches and styles within schools are discernible over the years. It is interesting to contrast with today's approach the image of a bygone age projected by Goodwin (1968, p. 32) quoted in Jones (1987, p. 43):

> ... a thoroughly good school is one where pupils apply themselves to their work and play with a steady and successful zeal. If this does not obtain, the Head must call the quality of his own leadership into the strictest question. The fault will almost certainly be there, not with the staff and less still with the pupils. Staff and pupils are what the Head makes of them. No good general has slack soldiers – that is what leadership is all about.

Today, the task of leadership is shared with a range of people (Gronn, 2000; Gunter, 2005). Goodwin's work describes that era of the 'monarchic Head' who was replaced by the 'bureaucratic' phase of headship that attempted to make the head some kind of chief executive and to add 'a business-like veneer ... to their charismatic and traditional characteristics' (Jones, 1987). This phase has been followed by attempts to 'democratise' schools and their management. This may have been threatening for many heads. Jennings (1978) rationalised the thrusts for democracy – although the head's apparent authority diminishes as procedures become more democratic and participation becomes widespread at all levels, his or her personal influence could well be greater.

This suggests that with participative management approaches there may be a greater need for leadership or appropriate forms of leadership rather than traditional management. HMI in England and Wales published *Ten Good Schools* (DES, 1977), indicating that in such schools:

> Emphasis is laid on consultation, team work and participation, but without exception the most important single factor in the success of these schools is the quality of leadership at the head ... Conscious of the corruption of power, and though ready to take final responsibility, they have made power-sharing the keynote of their organisation and administration. Such leadership is crucial for success and these schools are what their heads and staff have made them.

The former Strathclyde Regional Council, in *Managing Progress* (1986), endorsed participation and consultation but insisted that while the headteacher should 'consult widely, the power of decision remains with the headteacher'. This concept of participation in management, therefore, situates decision-making power in the individual, albeit having taken into account the views of others obtained through the process of consultation. At all levels of management, failure to clarify such distinctions can result only in frustration and discontent.

Leadership style can promote a sense of purpose or mission within individual establishments. Torrington and Weightman (1989, pp. 224–30) describe the tensions inherent in managing schools. They itemise the tensions between conflict and consensus; between autonomy and control and of which combined orthogonally offer four major ways (a quadrant model) of dealing with such tensions. Leadership is one of these ways:

Figure 2.2: Tensions in managing schools

They suggest (p. 229) that only three of these main styles may be appropriate, but make no claims for the pre-eminence of any particular style. For example:

> Prescription is appropriate where consistency is important. Leadership is helpful when there is uncertainty that can and should be dealt with quickly. Collegiality is useful when the full commitment of individuals is necessary.

John West-Burnham (1997) summarises the principal differences between leading and managing (Figure 2.3):

Figure 2.3: Distinctions between leadership and management

LEADING *is associated with*	**MANAGING** *is associated with*
Vision	Implementation
Strategic issues	Operational issues
Transformation	Transaction
Ends	Means
People	Systems
Doing the right things	Doing things right

Kotter (1996, p. 11) offers an even more succinct definition. He indicates that *leadership* is concerned with:

- establishing direction
- aligning people
- motivating and inspiring.

While *management* involves:

- planning and budgeting
- controlling and problem solving
- organising and staffing.

As noted above, there are relatively few specific empirical research-based studies of headteacher leaders in Scottish schools, but there have been important studies in other areas of the United Kingdom. Day *et al.* (2000, 44–53) in an important 360⁰ study of twelve effective schools (encompassing both primary and secondary sectors), provide important views and metaphors of leaders. These include captains of ships; multi-faceted diamonds; film directors; servant leaders; team players. These headteachers suggested that leadership involved:

- building and sustaining relationships
- self-belief
- providing direction
- sharing high expectations
- enabling and supporting others
- modelling
- advocacy
- networking
- being community focused
- being proactive and aware of external developments.

While they saw management involving recruiting suitable staff, monitoring school performance, and the unfailing promotion of professional development.

Day's headteachers identified a genuine tension in their practice between leadership and management, both of which they saw as necessary parts of their job. One head memorably commented on the difference between the two: 'management was concerned with running the ship' while leadership was concerned with 'setting the course' (p. 135).

Teachers (pp. 75–6) suggested to the research team that leaders provided a role model; an overview and direction for the school; established standards and made tough decisions; set an example; delegated; encouraged and motivated staff; recognised strengths and built on them; remedied identified weaknesses; were approachable and impartial; have vision; are concerned with developing the ethos of the school, and recognised that leadership is not invested in one person. For teachers in the study, management was more concerned with establishing structures to achieve the vision and the effective running and organisation of the school. Earley *et al.* (2001, p. 3) confirm that:

Headteachers, and others in leadership positions in schools, tend to think of their roles in terms of 'leading with a clear vision' and 'setting high expectations'. They make a distinction between 'leadership' and 'management' conceptually, if not always in practice.

This would appear to support Southworth's (1995b) earlier contention that traditional views of leadership and management still hold sway, particularly in primary schools where leadership is equated with the role of headteacher and is something which occurs outside the classroom and is concerned with systems and procedures. We have discussed the distributed nature of leadership that is now increasingly recognised, yet when discussing a four-country study (MacBeath, 1998) of what participants thought of school leadership, MacBeath and Mortimore (2000, p. 15) state that 'for Scottish and English schools leadership was uncontroversially represented in the person of the headteacher'.

Scottish HMIE, in their publication *Improving Leadership in Scottish Schools* (2001, pp. 4–5), suggest inspection evidence indicates 'that, in some schools, managers tend to over-emphasise the day-to-day administrative functions of their roles rather than giving sufficient attention to the key aspects of providing more strategic leadership'. While recognising that leadership and management skills are complementary and closely linked, 'strategic' is the key word in that HMI analysis:

- Leadership, therefore, is closely related to strategic management but distinguishable from more operational and administrative management tasks in a number of key respects:
- Leadership is about setting out and inspiring others with a longer-term strategic vision for the future; without such leadership, management tends to have a narrow and restrictive focus on the day-to-day.
- Leadership is about challenging and changing some of the key priorities; without such leadership, management tends to focus more on the best use of available resources to meet a specific priority.
- Leadership is about setting and reviewing objectives in relation to a clear strategic view of what is to be achieved; without such leadership, management may focus mainly on setting up systems to take forward particular objectives without questioning their appropriateness.
- Leadership involves winning hearts and minds and inspiring others to want to perform consistently to the highest standards; without such leadership, management may be more concerned with setting out and monitoring operational guidelines which

restrict innovation and creativity rather than empowering staff to perform.

- Leadership involves looking beyond the school and working with others who can contribute to school improvement; without such leadership, management may tend to evaluate success against a limited and inward-looking view of what is possible.
- Leadership sets out and builds an over-arching school ethos of achievement and success; without such leadership, management may focus only on means of monitoring and tracking performance, without promoting improvement.

Through a series of professional development and activities and case study examples from schools, teachers and headteachers are encouraged to evaluate the state of leadership within their own schools and to establish targets to improve. In this view, leadership quality can be enhanced by management processes.

HMIE (2007b) provided an updated perspective on leadership, particularly in relation to 'leadership for learning'. This publication provides strong messages, and key points about the importance and focus of leadership across educational sectors supported by illustrations gleaned from a limited consideration of the leadership literature and from their own inspection processes, evidence base and reports.

Governments and policy makers have an ever-increasing faith in the capacity of leadership to effect educational change. The search for improved and more effective schools with an associated rise in student attainment is often reliant on the capacities of individual heads or leaders. The school effectiveness and school improvement literature of the past twenty years, well summarised in MacBeath and Mortimore (2001), constantly emphasises the importance of school leaders, and broader sets of leadership skills. If school leadership has been 'for a purpose', the favoured political model of such purpose has been 'school improvement'.

Impact of school effectiveness and improvement movements

Over the past two decades, various factors in the 'effective' school have been identified and promoted in the context of a political will for schools to improve their performance. These factors include: developing a school climate and ethos with shared values; expert and skilled teachers having high expectations of and positive relationships with pupils; involving pupils purposefully in learning and providing an attractive work environment which illustrates pupil work. The burgeoning literature on school improvement and effectiveness has consistently identified leadership as a key element in the effective or improving school. Additionally government departments also make much of the role of the school leader, normally the headteacher (DES, 1977; Southworth, 1990; Murphy, 1991; Sammons *et al.*, 1995; Stoll and Fink, 1996; Dalin, 1998).

In Scotland, the quality and importance of school leadership and management in effective schools was repeatedly stressed by several influential reports (HMI, 1984; 1988; 1989) although the focus was largely on effective management. HMIE highlighted the shortcomings of the leadership of headteachers in around 15 per cent of schools in all sectors (HMIE, 2007b, p. iv). Similar degrees of weakness were identified for leadership at other levels of the school's organisation. This provides some of the background to the policy commitment to develop and implement a qualification and Standard for Headship in Scotland, discussed below.

Effective school leaders

The importance attributed to headship practice in blocking or supporting school improvement meant that alongside the research literature on school effectiveness, a literature of leadership effectiveness has also developed. This research literature suggests that effective school leaders possess the capacity to generate a *vision* with associated objectives and can provide a map or means of how to achieve this – the *mission*. The most effective school leaders also combine these capacities with an inspiring and convincing articulation of their personal and professional values (MacBeath, 1998). Moral and ethical qualities and concerns, especially in the light of the tensions inherent in modern school leadership, guide both vision and mission. Dempster and Logan (1998, p. 96) suggest:

> developing the necessary self-confidence to withstand the stresses and strains encountered when external and internal priorities conflict is essential for the well-being of a modern principal. Refining, understanding and confirming the educational values that lie at the heart of consistent decision-making are important components of principals' professional learning. A set of professional values is necessary if principals are to mediate productive settlements in contradictory situations …

MacBeath and Myers (1999, pp. 54–7) cite a study involving 27 participating headteachers who categorise leadership style in three ways:

- collaborative and collegiate
- flexible and mixed
- strong and up-front.

Day *et al.* (2001) confirm these and suggests the addition of a fourth category:

- Good leaders are informed by and communicate clear sets of personal and educational values that represent their moral purposes
  for the school.

This emphasis on the individual leader should perhaps be tempered by
a reminder of the shared leadership themes outlined in the first part of this
chapter. Law and Glover (2000, p. 11) are quite clear about the capacity of
individuals:

> Ultimately, leaders and managers achieve little on their own, whether
> on the basis of charisma or hard work: effective managers and leaders
> are those surrounded by effective followers and collaborators.

While Sergiovanni (2001, p. 2) suggests:

> It is not by chance that some leaders are more effective than others,
> even when all are faced with similar demands and constraints.
> Effective leaders have a better understanding of how the worlds of
> schooling and school leadership work. They have figured out alter-
> natives to direct leadership that are able to get people connected to
> each other, to their work, and to their responsibilities.

Although leadership is shared in this way, it is the experiences of headteachers, those who want to be heads and those who decide it is too difficult to
lead from that position, which are the focus of the next chapter.

CHAPTER 3

EXPERIENCES OF HEADSHIP

This chapter draws on a series of Scottish studies to illuminate the contemporary practice of headship, and to enable comparisons to be made between the experience and practice of headship and the management and leadership literature. Drawing together ideas from the preceding chapters raises questions about the perceived role of the headteacher. What is expected of those who lead educational institutions, and how might they be best prepared for their task? Wong (2001) asks, 'What kind of school leaders do we need?' Is the Scottish tension between hierarchy, with its associated bureaucratic pressures and the democratic values, which are perceived as characteristic of Scottish schooling, a healthy constructive one? How is the task of leadership perceived and experienced? Do school leaders expect and find autonomy to develop their schools with their colleagues or are they constrained by a bureaucratised and highly centralised system within which they find little room for manoeuvre or real decision-making? The answers to these questions have significance for the recruitment and retention of headetachers as well as implications for the most appropriate ways in which new heads may be prepared for their responsibilities.

Investigating expectations and experiences of headship

How is headship regarded, how attractive is it, how many plan to seek it? At a time when teachers' working arrangements are changing, what is known about the current experience of headship?

In order to offer answers to these questions, findings from a series of studies of Scottish headship will be explored, including:

- a group of 14 early retiring headteachers
- 87 depute headteachers in primary schools
- a smaller group of 10 deputy headteachers in secondary schools
- 37 new heads of primary schools
- a smaller group of 10 new heads in secondary schools
- acting headship in primary and secondary schools (64 acting heads and 24 local authorities)
- a survey of 153 secondary heads and deputes
- a study of headteacher dilemmas.

The findings will be reviewed in the light of further research in and beyond Scotland and the OECD reports of 2004 and 2007 (OECD, 2004; 2007).

The changing role of the headteacher: experiences of early retiring heads

It is generally recognised that the role of headteacher has changed, with a move from educational leading professional to manager (Hellawell, 1991; Menter *et al.*, 1995) and subsequently, with a focus on leadership to managing leader, headteachers are expected to satisfy demands of a wider range of stakeholders than hitherto: not only local authorities and the Inspectorate, but also parents, local businesses and more (Jones, 1999). How were these changes experienced by headteachers themselves?

Fourteen primary headteachers were interviewed a few months after their (early) retirement and invited to talk about their experience of headship and their decision to retire (Draper and McMichael, 1996). They spoke about both the losses and the gains associated with leaving the post, highlighting the loss of positive relationships that they had valued, the loss of the role, the status and the challenge. They had found the changes in headship very challenging.

They had experienced a significant change in the role and referred to vastly increased paperwork and bureaucracy. Earlier in their tenure it had been *their* school and *their* children, but this sense had been lost as control was centralised. These headteachers felt they had lost control of their time and their schools. Some were dissatisfied with the way the post had narrowed, although others had perceived a broadening. Some had seen their authority diminish as others gathered strength and influence. As Wallace and Huckman (1996) suggested, participation and collaboration with those in and beyond the school which may empower recipients may simultaneously disempower heads. The headteachers also reported less autonomy in relation to their education authority and had found they were no longer as able to respond appropriately to local events and conditions. The McCrone Report (SEED, 2000b) urged a shift in emphasis in the education system towards acknowledging teachers as autonomous professionals. Such intended increased autonomy may accrue to headteachers but autonomy, like decisions, may be a limited entity which at best can be shared round. The OECD report of 2004 signalled the commitment to increased autonomy for schools. The 2007 report suggests that while schools now appear to have more scope about their activities, there remains pressure to prioritise multiple policy initiatives simultaneously, leaving schools little scope to make demands manageable. It remains to be seen whether such a shift in autonomy can be achieved within a context which continues to emphasise compliance and target-setting at national level in many ways.

Aspiring to headship?

Given such a view of headship, who would wish to be a headteacher, and why? Did potential headteachers of the future see headship as the retired headteachers had experienced it? A study of 87 primary deputy headteachers threw some light on their views on headship. (Draper and McMichael, 1998a). The group, who responded to a survey, mostly had wide experience in a range of posts and schools. They had broad leadership and management experience. Most saw themselves as ready for headship. It was a real decision therefore when they were considering whether or not their career plans included applications to become a head. They had enough experience to apply and the question was whether or not they would.

A common assumption is that people will go as far as they *can* in career terms and this view is frequently held by senior managers who themselves have made ambitious choices in their careers. Insufficient account may be taken of those who could go further but choose not to – those who go as far as they *wish* rather than as far as they can. Clearly there are reasons for such decisions:

> I'm glad I did acting headteacher, because it made up my mind that it wasn't for me.

> Although I feel I could cope with a headteacher post, it does not appeal to me because of lack of contact with the children, too much paperwork and bureaucracy (primary deputy head).

Converting potential headteachers into actual applicants for headship has proved problematical, in Scotland and elsewhere. OECD (2007) suggested that insufficient attention had been paid to identifying and addressing reason for declining applications for headship. The intrinsic nature of the role, the 'job design', appears to be problematical for a goodly proportion of those who might be identified as 'potential headteachers'. Having an informed and realistic preview of the post as in the case of acting heads and those taking the Scottish Qualification for Headship (SQH) may make for clearly informed decisions ... the triumph of experience over hope! While some have voiced concerns that some entering the SQH training route do not complete and that some potential heads don't apply (a concern we return to in the final chapter), this may be understood as a decision not to seek headship in the same way that some drop out of initial teacher education having identified that teaching is not suitable for them. Similarly with headship: if some become clear it is not for them, then it is surely better that this is realised before they seek headship?

The deputy headteachers in Draper and McMichael's study (1998a) were asked if they were 'very likely', 'fairly likely' or 'unlikely' to apply for headship and why. One third indicated they were 'very likely' to apply while a quarter were 'fairly likely' to apply. The largest group, just over 40 per cent, were 'unlikely' to apply. Most agreed that they were ready for headship itself and for the responsibility it would bring, although a number did not wish to pursue the possibility. Their views were analysed using a prompt list of motivators and disincentives in relation to applications for headship. There were very similar ratings for the motivators. They agreed that heads could introduce their own ideas and that heads could control the agenda rather better. Commenting further on the incentives, respondents highlighted the following:

> ... the challenge of being in charge ...

> ... its being able to implement your own ideas and with devolved management you can apply your mind to new ventures ...

> ... a unique chance for creative employment ...

Southworth (1995b) reported headteachers' feelings of power and influence, which suggests that headship may well meet their expectations. This perception that headship brought significantly increased power to impact on the school process suggests that the model of democratisation highlighted in Chapter 2 has some way to go in that the responses did not highlight engaging with the views of others.

There was real awareness of the costs associated with headship. Asked to advise a friend thinking of applying for headship, the potential heads replied:

> Think about whether you are willing to sacrifice personal and family time to the degree required.

Two points are relevant here: firstly that the quotation reflects an assumption that the headteacher has little agency in the role; that compliance with demands is the only possible route. The second issue is that of whose sacrifices are being predicted. The Australian study (ASPA et al., 2003) highlighted that sacrifices were not restricted to the heads themselves, but included their families' lives also. Two-thirds of the heads studied believed their families suffered as a consequence of their work commitments. Families were identified by many as a key source of support, along with senior colleagues. This was particularly important in that support from employers was frequently lacking, a phenomenon which was characteristic of the Scottish findings also.

Further responses from potential heads in the Scottish study yielded concerns about specific demands of the role and the importance of making an informed decision:

The greater financial responsibility is the most important discouragement ...

Don't! Caution her to think very carefully ...

The potential heads varied more over disincentives, agreeing what they were but holding different views about their importance. 'Very likely' applicants were much less deterred by the perceived high level of workload, the extensive bureaucracy and paperwork, the demanding level of accountability and the financial responsibilities which they often considered part of the post. They were less put off by what they regarded as inevitable quality of life consequences such as loss of relationships. For those 'very likely' to apply the disincentives associated with headship mattered little:

> Make sure you know what the job entails, be sure it's what you want, be prepared for the hassles and grow another skin.

> Be prepared for shocks. Don't change too much too fast. Your new staff will be talented professionals ... keep thinking this even after you discover it's not true!

For those planning to apply, the disincentives were seen as part of headship and to a considerable extent also as part of the job they currently held as deputes. In comparison, those who were unlikely to apply saw headship as more distinct from their current post, with additional responsibilities and activities and personal costs which they judged as unattractive.

Were these views peculiar to primary deputes, or were they shared by secondary deputes? A group of 10 secondary deputes were interviewed (Draper and McMichael, 1998c). Half were unsure whether or not they would apply, the other half confidently expected to apply provided suitable opportunities arose. When considering applications, however, they would almost all be highly selective. They intended to apply only to schools which they judged were right for them in terms of their experience and personal circumstances. They were looking for schools where their past experience would be of value in helping them establish their credibility as leaders, and candidates who would be successful in post. For almost all of them it was *not* the case that any headship would do. This may help to explain why some headteacher vacancies are more difficult to fill than others, although potential applicants were concerned to build on their own successful past experiences and the types of schools involved would vary, as presumably would their choice of where to apply. It did not appear to be the case that all aspirant heads would be likely to apply for the same posts.

> I would be choosy about headship, but I know now where to apply (secondary)

> Go only for the job you want (secondary)

Primary aspirants agreed:

> Consider the character of the particular school: choose your school carefully.

> Often you may apply for schools you may not really want but you need the experience. Think about what happens if you get the job.

Potential applicants judged that some schools with particular kinds of catchment areas or characters would not be suitable for them. They also recognised the time needed to prepare applications, including researching the schools in detail. Thus there was a limit to how many applications could be made. Applications would be made if the job looked better than they had at present. Many were fairly content in their depute head jobs and had considerable autonomy in their posts. They had their own projects in school and one of the effects of collaborative, participative management styles may be to reduce the need to be head in order to put their ideas into practice. It may not be worth the additional responsibility and pressure if the autonomy exists in the depute role. Amongst secondary staff, as in primary, there was agreement that motivators included introducing one's own ideas, having more control and being able to steer the agenda of change in a school. There was also agreement that the disincentives were paperwork and bureaucracy, greater accountability, the effect on quality of life, and on relationships with colleagues and pupils. Some clearly had experiences that helped their development:

> I am in the fortunate position to work as part of a senior management team who share all decisions and communicate openly. I am given every opportunity to use my past experience.

For those who did not, the mechanisms of subsequent support need to be watertight! Those who did not feel they had a clear view of the job or of how it might be done might be expected to be reluctant to apply:

> I have not built up the confidence to apply ... I am seldom consulted or informed about decisions important to the running of the school.

Potential headteachers were confident that they knew what headship would be like. They believed they were familiar with the job and some had had opportunities to prepare themselves. They did not believe the job would be straightforward or easy and they saw headship as a clear mix of positive and negative aspects, with inherent tensions. They based their career decisions upon their understandings of the role. How accurate and realistic were their ideas?

Realistic expectations? The experience of newly appointed heads

Kelly's (1980) GLAD model (Figure 3.1) is helpful for analysing the experiences of new heads. This model was originally developed to conceptualise the transition from work to retirement and has been found to be useful in considering a range of personal transitions, particularly in relation to work (Hayes and Nutman, 1981). Kelly's model emphasises that any transition involves gains and losses. Detachment gains are the positive benefits and detachment losses are the negative aspects of leaving the previous state. Attachment gains are the positive effects and attachment losses are the negative dimensions of the new situation.

Figure 3.1: Kelly's GLAD model

	Gains	**Losses**
Attachment	positive aspects of the new job	negative aspects of the new job
Detachment	benefits of leaving the previous job	costs of leaving the previous job

This model was used to analyse the findings from a study of recently appointed primary heads. Data were collected from 37 primary headteachers who had all been in post for less than three years. There was agreement that one of the detachment gains was stopping working to another person's agenda. It was good to get away from finding difficulties in generating change because they were not in charge. Many had felt their strengths had been underused as deputies and there were real benefits in moving to headship. Some of the expectations of deputies about headship are thus confirmed.

Detachment losses also reinforced the views of both early retiring heads and the aspiring deputy heads. One loss was in the quality of collegial relationships with pupils and colleagues. As headteachers, their relationships were framed by the role, which reinforces the image of Scottish schools as hierarchical bureaucracies rather than flatter, more organic structures. Further effects of leaving a familiar situation were the loss of a sense of competence, of knowing how the system worked, of knowing how to make the system work, of knowing how to ensure that desirable ends could be achieved. As a head in a new school system, they did not know the administrative procedures and they had found themselves wrong-footed at times.

Attachment gains included seeing school development happen, knowing that one had had a role in seeing planned developments occur and having some control over the direction of developments. Attachment gains also included personal development, for much new learning had taken place. There was involvement in a much wider professional world than had been the case as a deputy. There were bigger networks and wider systems of which one became a member, but there were also attachment losses. The headship burdens of paperwork, bureaucracy, accountability and losses in relationships and quality of life all featured in the accounts given by the new heads. As had been expected, there was less time for oneself than had been the case before. As Wilson and McPake (1999) found, this was especially the case for those who were teaching heads in small primary schools. Here there was multi-tasking and little scope to depend on colleagues in the early days. The new headteachers painted a picture of a complex job with many differing facets, some positive and some negative.

Louis (1980) suggested that, however well prepared one might be, there are always surprises when moving from one job to another. Surprises arise in the differences between what people expect a job to be like and how the job is actually experienced. Primary headteachers were asked what had surprised them in their post and they reported with feelings about role overload (Draper and McMichael, 1998b). Although they had known that there would be much paperwork, they had not realised that the mountain would be so large. Nor had they realised the speed of decision-making that would be required or some of the difficulties inherent in being in charge:

> Be prepared to be unpopular with at least one member of school staff at any one time.
>
> It can be lonely at the top.

Garrett and McGeachie (1999) found that many deputy heads do not find opportunities for professional development within their work and that some are unable to develop a strategic perspective, but think mainly in operational terms. This finding suggests that headship involves a change of mindset, but when new headteachers feel highly pressed this will be difficult to achieve. Draper and McMichael (1998b) found primary headteachers had expected to take decisions but had expected to have time to make *informed* decisions and time to consider a range of alternatives. In practice they found themselves having to take decisions very quickly with little information which inevitably led to later regrets. They described role conflict as well as role confusion, struggling with conflicting obligations to their colleagues and parents, to pupils, to staff, and to senior staff. Like their Australian counterparts, they were frustrated by finding little time and space for important initiatives. In addition, there was conflict between the job and their personal commitments. Again this is echoed in the Australian study where one headteacher remarked 'I have no personal life – its starting to have an impact.' Such difficulties have significant implications for retention, as well as recruitment, as Williams noted (2003).

Although they had expected their working relationships to be different, they had also been surprised by the responses of others. They were surprised to receive respect from colleagues simply by being the head, although they were conscious that they might lose it in time if they did not subsequently earn it. The aspirations of the McCrone Report (SEED, 2000b) towards teachers becoming and being acknowledged as more autonomous professionals have signalled a potential change in this culture of deference; however, such aspirations are less evident in the subsequent agreement (SEED, 2001a) and thus the opportunity for their implementation seems less likely. The new heads were also surprised by how careful they had to be about what they said and to whom they said it, having found that what they said was repeated elsewhere and became understood as policy.

Some were also surprised by the absence of education authority interest. There had been considerable involvement of education authority staff at the point of recruitment and selection, followed by some induction into post, but subsequently for many all was quiet unless there was a problem. They were surprised not only by the responses of people but also by their own activities. They were shocked by how little time there was to monitor classrooms. They had envisaged such monitoring as a core part of the job, yet they found themselves with little time for it. Finally, they were surprised by the need to understand and work with new systems. However, they had also developed coping strategies and there were good experiences which they positively appreciated:

> It's never boring!
>
> Concentrate on what you have achieved at the end of the day, not what you haven't.

This focus on being proactive appears as a successful coping strategy in the Australian study (ASPA *et al.*, 2003) and is in sharp contrast to the reactive compliance with which many approached the overload issue. Deriving satisfaction from what is going well and from a sense of doing one's best are both identified as approaches which make the job more manageable.

Do these views match the views of secondary headteachers? Draper and McMichael (2000) interviewed a smaller sample of 10 new secondary headteachers who worked in a rather different way to their primary counterparts. Their responses suggested that their main concern as heads of large secondary schools was to create a context in which effective teaching and learning could take place, but in doing this they had to negotiate contexts that already existed. Existing contexts in the school could not be magically reshaped into what they wanted.

> You need to think very carefully about your first meetings with staff … (to say) there are things I'd like to do but I need to know what you want to do …
>
> Don't forget what it's like to be in the classroom, especially with a difficult class.

The context was in part set by the previous headteacher and his or her way of operating and the expectations and learned responses that followed from the previous incumbent's style. The context was also influenced by staff expectations and attitudes, as well as by staff strengths and areas for development. The senior management team, explored particularly by Wallace and Hall (1994) and Wallace and Huckman (1996), was a further feature of the context. For some, it included people who had applied for the headship and for all it had its own unique working dynamics which first had to be understood before seeking to negotiate changes in practice. This tension reflects the sensitivity to managing people which Hay McBer (2000) found to be more characteristic of educational than business managers. Some had been able to build a close link with their deputy, similar to the 'leadership couple' described by Gronn (1999). Where this bonding had been possible, new headteachers had found it invaluable. There was also the context provided by other headteachers which offered the support, ideas, suggestions about the ways things were done, and finally the context operated by the education authorities.

These new headteachers felt well prepared by their past experiences and they had been in management in secondary schools for quite some time. They did not expect headship to be plain sailing but to be testing as well as rewarding. However, they also reported surprises, including the amount of time they spent on administrative rather than educational matters and the rush of work relentlessly combined with accountability. They were quite prepared to be accountable, but they had expected to have time to shape the things for which they found themselves accountable. They found themselves less able to influence what happened than expected and yet far more accountable than they had been in the past. Some were very surprised by the poor discipline in schools and a further area of surprise was parents. Schools had very different kinds of parents and the issues that were of greatest concern to parents varied from school to school to a greater extent than they had expected. Finally, like their primary counterparts and as Mercer (1996) also found, they were surprised by the isolation and loneliness of the post, even when senior management colleagues and other colleagues were interested and supportive. The buck stopped with them. There were a number of issues that only they could deal with and they felt to a greater extent than they had expected that they were on their own in dealing with these.

Murphy (2003) conducted a postal survey, which was responded to by 153 Scottish secondary heads and deputes, including over 25 per cent of serving headteachers and a smaller proportion of deputes. The survey, which was based on a similar survey of New Zealand and Australian school principals (Cranston et al. 2003), provides some interesting insights into the challenges and tensions of a changing role. Key findings were:

- *role overload*: secondary school leaders were challenged by the quantity of the demands made on them; for the vast majority this leads to 50+ hours each week, and for a large number of these over 60 hours;
- *competing demands*: those surveyed said that operational and reactive management – dealing with the managerial/bureaucratic demands of the system and reacting to situations in the school community which demand a response – takes up too much of their time. They therefore could not spend as much time as they would like on the strategic and educational aspects of their leadership role;
- *professional development*: while welcoming professional development opportunities, and looking forward to higher quality development in the years ahead, they believed that no matter how much professional development there was, there was still too much to do;
- *satisfaction*: despite their worries, the overwhelming majority derived great satisfaction from their work and felt that they made a difference by what they did;
- despite their high satisfaction levels, respondents were concerned about some aspects of the *policy framework* in which they worked: for example, they showed concern about the implications of the national agreement governing teachers' pay and conditions for pastoral care in schools (since previous arrangements for 'guidance' posts were changed) and for professional progression (given the reduction in the number of promoted posts); they were also anxious about their ability to deliver on 'inclusion'.
- respondents had varied views on the *role of local authorities*, with only around half believing that the local authorities for which they worked added value to the work of the school, or promoted better joint working;
- interestingly in the light of the *political context* of their work outlined in Chapters 1 and 2, the survey made clear that school leaders saw themselves much more as 'professionals' than as 'local authority middle managers'.

Several issues are raised by these studies. The image and experience of isolation sits oddly alongside Gronn's work on distributed leadership (2000) and Wallace and Huckman's (1996) and Wallace and Hall's (1994) work on the importance of senior management teams in making schools work. Gronn suggests that in fact most leadership is distributed in practice and the papers on senior management teams suggest they are necessary for schools to operate effectively. The isolated headteacher image does not fit these conceptions of leadership. Reeves *et al.* (1997), however, highlight that as part of the settling-in process headteachers may find they have to 'fight their way in' with staff who are 'wary and watchful' before they become fully accepted in their role. Moreover, many studies of headship, for example Murphy (2007, pp. 19–23), identify a persistent theme of personal stress and emotional intensity. Gronn (2003) believes that the emotional intensity of the job has increased greatly as the political and managerial demands on schools have increased. He coins the memorable phrase 'greedy work', work which becomes the 'measure of what one is, not just what one does' (p. 153), to highlight the impact these emotional pressures can have on a headteacher's identity. Murphy (2007) argues that it is often the collision of the tensions and paradoxes of contemporary schooling in individual cases, 'dilemmas', which can cause particular pressure. For Dempster and Berry (2003), school principals dealing with such dilemmas are 'blindfolded in a minefield'. Duignan and Collins (2001, p. 132) had similar findings:

> heads reported that they often felt alone, cast in the role of arbiter or mediator relying on personal values and professional ethics to find a morally defensible solution.

Other issues relate to familiarity with the post, surprises that inevitably come with a new post and the extent to which people can be prepared for these surprises ahead of time. These findings have implications for preparation both in terms of experiential learning opportunities and formal training. The importance of induction is emphasised. There is also the issue of the balance that heads have to strike between innovation and integrating into and working with the staff team. None said they could just go in and change things. All had to work with existing circumstances and there was a real tension between doing things their own way and taking people with them. Such findings offer insights into expectations about, and early days in, headship. A balance must be achieved between being proactive and seeking to shape and focus activity and working with the current views, ways of working and aspirations of colleagues. The Australian study suggested it was important for heads to be proactive and to make the job manageable by setting priorities, but if these priorities are very different from those of colleagues then it may be very easy to lose the support of staff. Similarly heads may find they have to change themselves and their ways of working: as one Australian head recounted: 'I used to be perfectionist but that was unhealthy; now I do my best and I'm satisfied with that.' Initial preparation for headship and early support systems for headship need to acknowledge and address these issues.

Acting headship: an extreme case?

The study on acting headship (Draper and McMichael, 2002; 2003) raised a number of quite separate questions but also reflected many of the findings above.

The current emphasis on effectiveness and the importance of school leaders in sustaining and developing standards assumes that headships are relatively long-term positions. The study of acting headship was undertaken in two parts. The first phase was a survey of local authorities about acting headship, including how many acting headships there were, why these posts came about and how acting headteachers were selected. Three-quarters of the local authorities responded. In the second phase, data were collected about their experiences from staff who had held acting headships. The methods used were interviews with a small number and a survey of 64 staff. In the year studied one tenth of schools had been run by acting headteachers. Two types of acting headship were apparent: those (two-thirds) where the head was temporarily absent and expected to return and those where the head had left permanently and a replacement was awaited. The main reasons for temporary acting headships were illness and secondment. Headteachers became permanently absent due to retiral, resignation and, a much smaller third cause, promotion. The majority of the acting headships had been expected to last for under three months. Significantly the duration of these posts, however, was often exceeded, as in the case of one who said 'three weeks became two years'. One-quarter had not been defined at all, even at the initial point of creation.

Well over half the appointments were sudden. While it is to be expected that some acting headships would arise very suddenly, for example due to illness, others like secondments and promotions could have involved a greater degree of planning than was evident. Most acting headships were filled internally and automatically by the next person in line. However, 30 per cent were external appointments. Perhaps surprisingly, external appointments were as likely for short periods of acting headship as they were for long. Summarising their experience of headship, those who had been (or still were) acting headteachers reported that the preparation arrangements for acting headship, for induction and for support, were generally weak, although there were notable exceptions. On the whole, however, they had to fall back on their own past experience and advice from absent heads, if available. These were the most helpful sources of continued support. Uncertainty over length of time and scope caused difficulties. Not knowing how long they would be acting headteachers made it difficult to plan ahead and some were uncertain about the extent of their authority and the extent to which they could introduce radical change. The appointment arrangement of automatic promotion suggested that familiarity with the school was valued and a safe pair of hands was wanted to maintain the school in a time of staff changes. However, to half of the acting headteachers it had been indicated that they should introduce change even over short periods of time. This expectation is not surprising in a period of rapid change in the system, when schools cannot stand still but are expected to keep moving forward, but it did mean that acting heads faced conflicting expectations.

Staff believed a period of acting headship was helpful in securing experience which would contribute to a stronger application for subsequent headship and it is therefore important that these opportunities are equally available to all those who might be interested. Preparation and induction were raised, yet again. One local authority in the study had created a pool of acting headteachers, who had volunteered and been selected into the pool and who were given some preparatory training. Should they have to take over a school at short notice they would be at least partially prepared. This process is now in use in several authorities. Management of the ending of the acting post was also an area of concern. Two-thirds of those acting reverted to their previous post when headteachers returned. This reversion could be difficult and sensitive. Some watched as the changes they had put in place were systematically dismantled.

Those who had held acting headships reported a considerable degree of freedom in post. This was in sharp contrast with the English situation as described by Webb and Vulliamy (1996), who found that the growth of managerialism had reduced scope for autonomy. Many of the acting headteachers had been able to make changes, appoint new staff, and take the school in their chosen direction. Acting headship was seen by them as an opportunity for professional development, for new learning, stimulation and challenge, which they felt had made considerable demands on them.

The majority felt positive towards future headship. In terms of career plans, 17 per cent had decided on the basis of their experience as an acting head that they would not apply for a permanent headship, but the rest intended to apply and a proportion had indeed already applied in the first few months after the completion of the acting post.

There are similarities as well as differences between the experiences of acting heads and those appointed to permanent headships. Differences relate to appointment procedures and equal opportunities, conflicting expectations held of acting headteachers and uncertainty over length of time and scope, the balance of freedom and limitations in post and the management of the ending of an acting headship. Similarities include concern over insufficient preparation, induction and support. The work on acting headship thus throws into relief many of the issues raised earlier. It highlights the need for careful selection, preparation, induction and support with due attention to professional development in order to protect and support both the new head and the school in times of major change. It also reveals a conflict between the perception of headship as key to school performance and, in some areas, a rather cavalier disregard for creating conditions in which acting headteachers might be expected to cope and flourish.

The importance of preparation, induction and support

Nicholson and West (1988) offer a four-stage model of induction into managerial posts: preparation, encounter, adjustment and stabilisation.

The first stage, preparation, covers the period from initial exploration of the vacancy by the candidate to the point of taking up the appointment. Adequate provision of appropriate information and support during this stage offers a realistic preview of the job and enables informed decisions to be made by both the candidate and selectors on suitability for the post. The second stage, encounter, encompasses the early days in post when initial impressions are formed and a rudimentary map of the setting is constructed. Again, effective support at this point helps to protect against major early mistakes and enhances the chances of early success which in turn has been found to be helpful both in speeding up the settling in process and in retention. The third stage, adjustment, may take six months to a year or more until the job and its setting have become more familiar ground and the understanding of role and context are much more deeply established. Useful support during adjustment derives from a continuing recognition that the person is relatively new in post. The final stage of stabilisation is reached when the person has settled in to the post to the point when he or she is ready to innovate and to look ahead. Once stabilised, heads can more readily refine their performance. Nicholson and West's work emphasises that, even given effective preparation, good induction and continuing relevant support is still needed. Applying this model to headship, the early experiences of the new headteachers outlined above suggest that for school managers there is still considerable room for improvement after appointment.

Reeves *et al.* (1997) similarly outline stages inherent in initially settling into a headteacher post (up to 2 years) to feeling thoroughly settled (4–10 years). They show the need for preparation, induction and support in the early period but also emphasise that development continues, as does the need for development opportunities and continuing support.

On the basis of this exploration the experiences of potential and new headteachers it is clear that the post of headteacher is complex and fraught with competing tensions and expectations: for example to innovate/integrate; to lead/support and even to lead/manage. These tensions may be avoidable or may be intrinsic to the job: if the former, then good preparation, induction and support may mean they can be avoided; if they are intrinsic, then at best they may be ameliorated by effective familiarisation, preparation, induction and continuing support. A first step in either case is to map out the territory conceptually as well as experientially.

Experiencing headship: tensions and dilemmas

Published first-person accounts of headship (Ribbins and Marland, 1994; Tomlinson *et al*, 1999) are now complemented within the literature by the wide variety of field research into the experience of headship discussed above. Several studies (MacBeath, 1998; Day *et al.*, 2000; Duignan and Collins, 2001; Moller, 1996; Ehrich *et al.*, 2006; Cuban, 1996; Begley, 2004) report on the tensions and dilemmas of headship. In part these tensions of a caring professional service arise from the challenges and paradoxes of contemporary schooling policy, with its competing demands for care and efficiency. Duignan (2001) uses the concept of 'The Managed Heart' (taken from seminal studies by Hochschild (1983)), to clarify some of the issues. Duignan argues that there is a current emphasis in many caring organisations and services, including schools, on rationalist styles of management, which emphasise concepts and practices associated with efficiency, clear objectives, service standardisation and routines. He believes that emphasis represents an 'organisational pathology' which 'attacks both the 'hearts of organisations and of the people who work in them' (Duignan, 2001, p. 33). He goes on:

> Leaders … are expected to invest more than their knowledge and skills to effectively discharge their responsibilities in contemporary organisations. Emotional involvement and a deep commitment to their relationships, their organisation, and their work is essential if they are to be regarded as credible.

Duignan argues that these tensions can be handled without damage if the sources of attack are understood and there is acknowledgement of the emotions such tensions generate. While this 'emotional labour' requires a degree of self-awareness for all teachers in schools, he argues it is a particular requirement of those who take leadership roles. He calls for 'leaders to acknowledge their own and other's feelings, emotions and passions' (p. 38). This self-awareness of the role of feeling in balancing the impersonal rationalities of scientific management fits closely with the work of Beatty (2000), who contrasts the behaviours and appearances which leaders and teachers in schools believe they need to exhibit and those which they need to acknowledge as 'fully dimensional human beings'. Beatty argues that the language of professional preparation and practice speaks of 'control' and 'managing emotions'. Within such a perspective, emotions may be seen as a threat to the smooth and orderly running of the organisation. Failure to acknowledge the emotional dimension of leadership may be costly to the individual and to the organisation in the long run. Headship involves managing conflicting demands which cannot all be satisfied, as well as reactions to their decisions. This pressure has costs for the individual which may impact on self-esteem, coping capacity and degree of engagement. Beatty argues that the character of schools as organisations requires emotional engagement, not detachment. The day-to-day experience of schools and schooling involves many human interactions. Thus, those accepting leadership positions are required to undertake 'emotional labour', which can be very demanding, sometimes draining. In this situation, self-knowledge and an ability to contextualise, understand, accept and develop the emotional character of their school experience is vital.

Beatty's study (2000) showed that teachers' interactions with the school principal, in particular interactions concerning career, had a strong emotional character. School leaders therefore need not only to understand their own emotions, but understand and be sensitive to the emotional impact which their power and position can have on others. She concluded from her research that the principal could 'have a powerful, direct and indirect influence on the growth and development of each teacher'.

If school leaders had only to pay attention to the emotional impact of their decisions and directives on the individuals involved, the role would be challenging enough, but such interactions often take place against a backcloth of competing and contested purposes and values. These give rise to genuine dilemmas, where, whatever is decided, one or other of the parties involved will suffer. Two other studies (MacBeath, 1998; Day *et al.*, 2000) independently identified such dilemmas as one of the key experiential features of headship. Day and his colleagues elaborate on three leadership dilemmas (pp. 146ff.):

Development versus dismissal
What do I do with a member of staff whose poor teaching is having an adverse effect on the education of the pupils and whose performance doesn't seem to be improving no matter what I do in terms of support and staff development?

Power with or power over?
... based around the tensions created in developing a clear vision for the school based upon existing sets of core values held by the headteacher and building a cohesive staff team ... not all of whom may share these values.

Subcontracting versus mediation?
... many of the headteachers in the study found themselves caught between two sets of imperatives for changes – internal and external. The external impetus for change was the 'imposed' changes (e.g. DfEE, Ofsted or the LEA) ... internal imperatives on the other hand were a complex mixture of school-based factors ...

MacBeath and his co-researchers looked for similar themes across the four countries in which they investigated leadership. One of the key conclusions was that 'leaders are often faced with contradiction' (Moos and Dempster, 1998, pp. 108–9). 'Living with contradiction so that professional integrity and self-worth are maintained is a prominent feature of contemporary leadership.'

Surprisingly, their research suggested that 'heads are increasingly meeting these types of situations and are often left alone to manage as best they can'. Dempster and Mahoney (1998) found that these situations could also often be characterised as 'dilemmas'. They saw some dilemmas (such as how to handle budget cuts or how to be 'competitive' in a market-driven school system) as arising from external forces, and some (such as the conflict between parents' desires for speedy resolution of complaints and teachers' rights to 'due process' which might be time-consuming) as internal to the school community.

In their discussions with us, heads reported that they often felt alone, cast in the role of arbiter or mediator relying on personal values and professional ethics to find a morally defensible solution. (p. 132)

Murphy (2002), in a study of dilemmas of practice within the Scottish secondary school system, found that headteachers saw the resolution of dilemmas as involving both short-term and long-term factors. These were:

- general long-term approaches to the head's role which would lead to a pay-off in particular situations (for example consistency of approach, developing sensitive antennae);
- personal integrity and character (seen, for example, in the fact that people in the school community would 'know what you stood for');
- systematic problem-solving approaches (be creative, seek solutions);
- working through the dilemma with those involved.

This last area was particularly interesting. Several of the headteachers interviewed believed that dilemmas were often resolved through the parties involved arriving at mutual understanding of context and issue and through their trust of both the process and the professional practice involved. This meant that the headteacher had to be open to and try to understand all the points of view, the facts and the values brought to bear by the different parties to the situation, but beyond that might play a key educational role in helping those involved to see the dilemma within a wider context of competing interests, irrational policy paradoxes, community priorities and values. Headteachers in this study talked of living with the tensions associated with dilemmas, and, echoed the findings of Beatty's earlier research, of 'holding onto the tension', 'working the tension' and 'holding things together'.

Dilemmas for school headteachers do not just arise within school settings. In an in-depth investigation of the relationship between secondary headteachers and their supervisors within education authorities, Cowie (2001) found that the greatest strains and tensions experienced by the headteachers in the study were not to do with their relationships within schools, but with local authority supervisors.

Many of the issues of emotional and ethical challenge involved in these experientially based accounts of headship practice can be found across the teaching profession, and other caring professions. However, those who assume leadership roles, even using the broad definitions of leadership identified in Chapter 2, experience these tensions in a greater measure, as they are involved in highly significant personal interactions. They make decisions which impact on a wider body of individuals, directly or indirectly, and in their own professional behaviour they exemplify a set of core values which are associated with the organisation as a whole. In this respect, school leaders are not alone. Kakabadse and Kakabadse (1999) found that in apparently more managerially dominated, impersonally framed, business environments, ethical dilemmas regularly challenge those in leadership positions.

The dilemmas in education often seem particularly compelling because they concern children in the process of formation. The decisions made will affect these children for life. There is a boy in school who is nearing the end of compulsory school, who loves working on his uncle's farm where he learns a great deal, but who has limited talent for formal reading and writing. Forced to continue to attend school, he expresses his increasing alienation in ways which disrupt the learning of others. Should the school leader connive at his increasing patterns of absence or use his or her authority to demand attendance? A girl is sexually assaulted at the weekend. The girl's parents arrive at school unannounced to declare that the school is failing their daughter as it continues to allow the boy whom she accuses of the assault (but who denies it) to attend the school. She has been so traumatised by the experience that she cannot possibly attend school while he is there. The school, they say, is therefore punishing their daughter twice – once in the assault, now by being denied her education. In a fuller analysis of these kinds of difficult challenges in professional practice, Murphy (2007) states that dilemmas must be approached through three different, but equally essential perspectives: the psychological, the political and the ethical. Each one of these perspectives has its own vocabulary, its own way of seeing what is at stake, but all three are needed if there is to be full understanding of the issue.

The psychological perspective has two important related aspects, cognitive and emotional. Cognitively, it is vital that the school leader understands the thinking processes that different individuals bring to a difficult dilemma. How do they see the problem? Are they open-minded and willing to learn? If the resolution of 'dilemmas' is often itself an educational process, those involved may need to be led to a new understanding. However, because of the 'high stakes' character of these situations for many of those involved, emotions may run high. These can interfere with cognition. It is important that the school leader can understand the emotional interplays affecting others, while also being able to deal with his or her own emotions. But a purely individual perspective on these interactions is often inadequate. The 'terms of engagement' may be set elsewhere. An understanding of the politics of the situation is always required.

The political perspective asks, in any situation, who has power and how are they using it? What constraints are imposed by the policy context in which this issue arises, by the legal requirements set nationally or by the conflicting interests or values of key players, such as the members of a school Parent Council or the locally elected Council. Diversity of values and interests within a school community can give rise to conflicts between key stakeholders, conflicts in which the different parties try to secure the headteacher's support for their 'side' of the argument. Moreover, school communities vary greatly in the 'social capital' on which they can call. In some communities, a strong sense of social trust derives from shared values and expectations. In others, trust may need to be established; there may be only a limited sense of ownership of, or engagement with, school-based education. School leaders need the antennae which will allow them to understand the different flows of power which can be found in their school community and take these into account in making decisions or supporting others to make decisions. But power without principle has no place in a democratic educational setting. This leads to the third perspective, that of ethics.

Ethical perspectives illuminate the rights and wrongs of a particular situation. What values and principles are in play? Are they in conflict? A common conflict in schools is between 'care' and 'rules'. In the study conducted by Duignan and Collins (2001), many Australian principals argued that following the rules too strictly disadvantaged some individuals. Rules offered guidance but individual decisions always had to be made. Others believed that the best protection for all was in consistency within the rules. For example, a school principal is quoted as having allowed a student, who had been disciplined, to participate in a major athletic activity even though the rules prohibited this. She thus put the principle of care (giving attention to the needs of the individual) over the principle of rules (ensuring consistent treatment for everyone who behaves in a certain way). In two other examples, however, school principals regretted placing care above rules. The rules, by being bent, had been weakened. They later 'believed (that) care-based choices were not the wise course of action for themselves. They should have followed the rules and would do so in future.' Yet had they kept to the rules, surely they would have been left with regret at the damage to the individual students involved. This is the very nature of dilemma and reflects the tension between equality, treating all the same and equity, treating according to need. Principles can sometimes work with each other, but sometimes are in conflict. Murphy concludes that the moral complexity of contemporary society requires school leaders who can make wise judgements in the complex situations they are likely to encounter.

Implications for preparation for headship

Halpin (2001) has highlighted the need for an increased role for human resource management in education. Headteachers' actual experience in post, both new and experienced incumbents, as well as deputies' perceptions of headship, seem remarkably distant from the developed conceptions of headship and leadership found in the literature. Certainly, the findings above suggest that, with the move from a predominantly educational to a more managerial role and beyond to a greater expectation of leadership, headteachers have a right to expect that their needs as managers and leaders will be recognised and provided for. The acting headship study paints a picture of suddenly appointed ill-prepared staff in schools being expected to sustain and develop schools with little induction and support. The broader research literature on the experience of headship suggest increasing tension and pressure, as more and more is expected of our schools and the headteacher is seen as the key figure in making this happen.

If headship is of paramount importance then should headteachers be treated differently? If one holds to a more distributed view of leadership then others in the school should also be involved and prepared, and heads should be less isolated. The research findings raise questions about the tensions between bureaucratic management roles and collaborative distributed leadership, both in perception and reality.

We should not be surprised if many decide they do not wish to take on the role, opportunities and responsibilities of headship. It may be that headship is coming to be perceived less as a prize and more as a professional obligation in which case incumbents will rightly expect more support and more realistic expectations and accountability mechanisms from the wide range of stakeholders. Murphy (2007) starkly highlights the conflicting expectations with which headteachers have to contend. In a policy context where concerns about work–life balance are becoming more prominent (ACAS, 2006; HSE, 2004), and litigation on work demands more common, a review of the role of headteachers could be credibly argued to be well overdue. Making unreasonable demands may finally bring its own rewards in recruitment and retention terms.

If school leadership is a serious endeavour it deserves a professional quality of planning, preparation and support, rather than being dependent on luck. This is not the same as central direction. Chapter 2 offered a scenario of more devolved school leadership, which should not be confused with central neglect or abandonment. The effective preparation of school leaders will be crucial if more devolved leadership is to become a force which enhances education. Initial preparation that helps people develop realistic expectations of the job and enables informed career decision-making is an important beginning, but continuing support and development will also be needed. Any design for preparation must lead into the provision of career-long continuing professional development for leaders as well as teachers in schools and needs to ensure an appropriate balance between socialisation and the development of the capacity to operate autonomously, between managerial competence and leadership. Do developments in leadership preparation meet such standards? We consider this in the following chapter.

CHAPTER 4

LEADERSHIP DEVELOPMENT

Introduction

It has been argued that school leadership is complex, constructed within a political model of service provision which in the Scottish context has limited the scope of leadership at school level and that within individual school communities leadership is shared in unpredictable ways which can cut across hierarchical or official position. It has also been maintained that, despite these restrictions, the potential for headteachers to influence the behaviour of others within a school community is considerable, although an excessive focus on the activities of management and administration can reduce leadership impact. It has also been shown that the conflicts, complexity and goal confusion of current schooling can lead to experiences of emotional challenge, tension and dilemmas of practice for those in leadership positions. This 'noise' around the job can obscure the bigger picture. Clearly, school leaders, and those who aspire to be school leaders and who share in leadership responsibilities, should participate in and benefit from development activities and challenges that encourage effective leadership practice. The research review has also suggested that, alongside common aspects of the experience and practice of leadership through headship, those at different stages of their career, for example, those newly appointed, will have particular needs related to their current situation. As schools in Scotland grope towards a flatter structure, with an acceptance of and encouragement of leadership at all levels, it is arguable that all those involved will need to be introduced to, and accept, their leadership responsibilities. Given that leadership operates at a variety of levels in the system, and is manifested in different roles, how is leadership to be developed?

Who needs development for leadership?

The discussion here will focus on headteachers because of their current crucial role in the system. Besides, that is where most of the structured activity within the Scottish system takes place. However, there are clearly implications for developing wider leadership abilities and understanding more widely. Leadership practice in school (as discussed in Chapter 2) involves management activity but also a broader range of abilities and capacities in:

- strategic thinking;
- interpreting and charting a way through complexity and change with and for others;
- locating the school within its broader social context;
- attracting followers, who are prepared to support and participate; and
- understanding and linking together the day-to-day activities of the school and its longer term purposes and values.

These abilities and capacities are shared within and among those associated with the school, and operate from different nodes and for potentially different purposes. It follows that many in the school community who participate in leadership will benefit from leadership development. The complex hierarchy of the Scottish school has obscured the key leadership role played by every teacher, no matter where he or she is placed on the flatter hierarchy (see Chapter 1). Student leaders, those with the capacity to influence and motivate their peers, may also benefit from development in leadership skills and concepts. Indeed, one could argue that all those who hold a stake in the school community, and therefore have the potential to play a leadership role, should be part of leadership development activity.

In this connection, it is worth recording our surprise that the Chartered Teacher development in Scotland under which all teachers have the opportunity to seek extended professional development through postgraduate study, issuing in Chartered Teacher status with enhanced pay, made no direct provision for development in leadership. Indeed, so suspicious were the teacher unions of the possibility that Chartered Teachers might be used to undertake management tasks within schools, that no programmes in leadership for Chartered Teachers, teachers who are likely to be the leading experts in teaching and learning in their schools, were to be developed. Growing concerns about the recruitment and retention of headteachers may encourage such developments in the future.

The Scottish system now recognises through the Improvement Framework developed in the Standards in Scotland's Schools Etc Act (SEED, 2000a) that leadership in schools is complex in its character. The agreement on teachers' conditions of service (SEED, 2001a, Annex D) requires that all teachers share in leadership decisions:

> All teachers will have the right to be fully involved in the development of the (school) plan and to be consulted on their contribution to the plan, and the responsibility for realising the school's development priorities.

Yet surprisingly little provision exists in Scotland for the development of leadership thinking, ideas and skills within the teaching profession. One may also argue for leadership development to support cultural renewal. New Community schools have yet to demonstrate that they provide different types of opportunities for more shared leadership development (O'Brien and MacLeod, forthcoming). Many professional and social barriers may have to be overcome in such schools. Multi-agency development of leaders and capacity, such as the development in Stirling of inter-agency training, may prove essential if this initiative is not to falter.

International leadership development

Scotland has much to learn from earlier developments in other countries. An early report on Primary Education in England and Wales, drawing on the evidence gathered by HMI, said very little about leadership but importantly stressed the role of the headteacher who:

> usually makes his [sic] staff feel that their views have due weight in decisions taken. The head must give a lead to his staff ... It is the Head's personality that in the vast majority of schools creates the climate of feeling – whether of service and co-operation or of tension and uncertainty – and that establishes standards of work and conduct. (DES, 1959, p. 92)

The important role of the individual head is clearly highlighted and reflects theoretical thinking of the time that leaders would have certain traits, or personality characteristics. This emphasis parallels a strong popular interest in the personality of those perceived to be successful headteachers. The larger-than-life headteacher has been a popular and appealing figure since modern schooling began. The famous Victorian head, Thomas Arnold, whose life story was used in the early part of the twentieth century as a key text in teacher training courses, is still recommended as a model for contemporary teachers in the twenty-first century (Copley, 2002). It could of course be argued that his fictional counterpart, Wackford Squeers, is both more famous and a truer representation of the dangers of concentrating power in one individual. Interest in successful individuals, however, continues to be a strong theme in the popular imagination. The *Times Educational Supplement* and other Scottish newspapers regularly provide sympathetic accounts of the positive impact which successful headteachers can have on a school, and through the school on a community.

There are various international interventions especially designed to prepare headteachers or principals, particularly in developed countries. Citing Joe Murphy's influential work (1992; 1998), when comparing developments in the USA and England, Brundrett (2001) suggests 'four distinct periods in the evolution of training programmes for school principalship in the USA' have been identified. These are summarised below:

Figure 4.1: Brundrett's periods in the evolution of training programmes for
school principalship in the USA

ERA	EMPHASES
Ideological 1870–1900	Role associated with teaching and instruction
Prescriptive 1900–45	Influence of Taylorism stressing technical and mechanical aspects of administration
Behavioural science 1945–1986	Management regarded as an applied science with significant university involvement
Dialectical 1986–	Major criticisms from government and society of failures of training programmes; universal standards and competences suggested for school leaders; complexity and paradox as themes.

Brundrett confirms that (as in Scotland) development programmes for
heads in England and Wales only emerged in the 1980s with an emphasis on
university MEds which were academically focused and many school leaders,
eschewing theory, saw little practical merit in such an approach. The 1990s
'saw a growing acceptance that skills developed in the workplace should be
seen as an integrated part of academic programmes ... which were flexible
enough to retain academic rigour whilst addressing the professional needs
of teachers'. Academic modular programmes, MBAs and professional doc-
torates emerged but at the same time practically focused training courses
in a plethora of DES-funded courses developed. The 1980s versions of such
provision were subsequently described as instrumental in nature.

Three elements of an increasingly centralised government strategy for the
improvement of leadership and management are identified by Brundrett:

- Headteachers' Leadership and Management Programme (HEAD-
  LAMP) (TTA, 1995a; 1995b), for newly appointed heads;
- National Professional Qualification for Headship (NPQH) (Bush,
  1998) for aspiring heads;
- Leadership Programme for Serving Headteachers (LPSH) (TTA,
  1998; Watkin, 2000).

This disparate set of activities was given coherence through the government-
funded National College for School Leadership (NCSL, see online) established in 2001 on the campus of the University of Nottingham.

Providers of HEADLAMP were approved by the Teacher Training
Agency (TTA) and had to focus on a catalogue of a TTA-defined 'tasks and
abilities' (the forerunners of competences) for headteachers. HEADLAMP
was thought to have strengths and weaknesses, including concerns about
the competence model and the notion that 'best practice' could be shared in
this way. An OFSTED (1998, p. 64) report declared:

it is clear that some headteachers who took part in the programme developed new skills and gained in confidence. On the other hand, there is as yet little clear evidence that many participating headteachers have made fundamental changes to their styles of leadership. There are also significant weaknesses in the quality of some of the training.

The NPQH, introduced in 1994, 'has had a chequered history in terms of the relevance of the assessment regime and the quality of the training programme through "private" consortia' (Reeves *et al.*, 2002, p. 31). NPQH was attacked for its reliance on competences and its approach to training and assessment (Bush, 1998; Riley, 1998a). Bush (p. 328) suggested that distinguishing between 'leadership' and 'management', the emphasis on 'best practice outside education' and the linkage between NPQH and specialist Masters' degrees in educational leadership and management all required further investigation. Other concerns indicate the continuing tension in NPQH; was it too academic or too practical without reflection? Such criticism led to a restructuring of NPQH, a re-launch in 2001 and the subsequent development of a wide range of 'leadership programmes' targeting professionals at different stages of career (NCSL, 2008).

Watkin (2000) describes The Leadership Programme for Serving Headteachers (TTA, 1998) initiative. Hay McBer's (2000) research into headteacher effectiveness and the resulting 'model of excellence' was applied to two key objectives in the LPSH – personal leadership development and school improvement. The associated 4-day programme involves *inter alia* assessment of personal leadership style, critical incident analysis, personal target setting and school improvement planning. Initial evaluations suggest the course is welcomed by many headteachers, for whom there has been a dearth of professional development opportunities.

In an authorative book, Gunter (2001, pp. 87–91) discusses the variety of approaches which have underpinned formal leadership development programmes world-wide. She identifies the two underlying issues as being what is to be learned and how adults in professional roles learn. She regrets the marginalisation of HEIs in England where the practical is emphasised and theory demonised, despite all that has been learned about propositional and procedural knowledge (Reeves *et al.*, 2002, pp. 13–14). With so many examples to draw on, what has been learned in Scotland?

Leadership and management development for Scottish schools

Scotland, as England, has had its fair share of strong characters who have inspired achievement or conflict, or sometimes both, within the educational communities they have led. The early stages of the development of comprehensive schools offered huge leadership challenges, as new headteachers had to forge a new vision and purpose for schools with, or against, their staff. Reflecting on this period, Paterson (2002) suggests that despite there being initially a logistical model for delivering comprehensive school buildings, and (later) a curricular model for providing greater equality of access to varied opportunities, Scottish education lacked a leadership model to accord with the structural design and the broad educational ambition of its comprehensive schools. The tasks of leading comprehensive schools were initially cast as managerial – creating timetables, managing resources – or narrowly curricular – organising courses and programmes of study.

R. F. Mackenzie, a popular and charismatic headteacher, brimful of good educational ideas, although perhaps politically naïve and lacking what would today be identified as some essential management skills, became embroiled in a terminal conflict with some of his own staff, his director of education and the Aberdeen education committee by refusing to compromise on his ideals (Mackenzie, 1995). The key point of conflict was the conditions under which corporal punishment should be administered in the school and eventually Mackenzie was suspended then dismissed from his post. Mackenzie's story was widely reported, and supported the view that ideal headteachers, appointed as officers of local education authorities and under the direction of directors of education, kept their schools out of controversy, away from public reporting of dissonance, by running tight and efficient organisations which complied with local and national advice. One well-known Scottish headteacher reported to one of the authors that the induction talk he received from the chair of the education committee in a central Scotland authority consisted of one short sentence. 'Never speak to the press and you'll be alright.' The consequent lack of 'shared knowledge', through neither publication nor the development of research interest in Scottish headship, has meant that learning about headship has perforce been on the 'craft' model, through individual character and lucky example. Models, centred on the personality and traits of the individual granted considerable powers of office, offered limited scope for developing leadership more widely.

Less controversial and difficult is the development of headteachers in management – essentially concerned with the effective and efficient implementation of policies decided elsewhere. HMI reports (HMI, 1984; 1988; 1989) encouraged leadership but also stressed management skills. SOED, local authorities, Teacher Education Institutions (TEIs) and schools invested in the 1980s in a wide range of management training initiatives, the most comprehensive of which was the government-funded suite of nine Management Training for Head Teachers (MTHT) modules in the early 1990s (SOED, 1990). SOED provided 75 per cent of the funding necessary to provide such modules in addition to producing the initial training materials. The programme to develop MTHT was a classic example of the then power of HMI and a centralised 'top–down' development approach. While selected headteachers were instrumental in the development of the various modules there was little overt general consultation. The programme reflected the dominant UK-wide 'delivery' approach to professional development of the times. Staff development was to be 'done to' headteachers and their senior teams. Dadds (1997, p. 32), arguing for a model of continuing professional development that promotes 'the development of teachers' understanding of learning, to their sense of voice, their judgement and their confidence to cultivate inner expertise as a basis for teaching and for judging outsider initiatives', describes such approaches:

> 'Delivery' or 'empty vessel' models of educational reform are, essentially, crude behaviourist models which assume erroneously that 'good practice' will come about from those outside schools making judgements for, and on, those inside.

The MTHT modules were best-practice oriented and covered a selection of available theory but stressed management more than leadership. They dealt with the key areas of principles of management, personnel, curriculum, resources, finance, monitoring and effectiveness, school and community, education and the law, and staff development and appraisal. These modules involved a mix of workshop, residential experience and individual school-based activities and study. Education authority advisers and headteachers who became trainer/tutors (Grant, 1995) worked in close collaboration with the TEIs and used government earmarked funds. Education authorities ensured that the take-up among headteachers and senior school personnel was significant. Additionally, education authorities began to develop a range of 'middle management' programmes that focused in secondary schools particularly on principal teacher development.

An evaluation of the MTHT programme suggested that it was found to be more useful by heads in primary than in secondary schools (Draper *et al.*, 1995). The reasons were perhaps because of scale or size or the extended experience many headteachers in secondary schools have as they progress through the school hierarchy. Another evaluation (Kerr, 1992) suggested that such programmes would have to be more directly related to a clear statement of the educational purposes of management activity and an analysis of the different management competences which headteachers required. Attempts were made to align such a programme with academic awards, an important example being Strathclyde Region's Management Development scheme (MANDATE), which accredited and certificated successful completion in partnership with local TEIs. While the MTHT initiative had only a limited success, the notion that aspiring headteachers in Scotland required to be trained and developed in leadership and management skills, abilities and values in the form of an appropriate qualification for the demanding post of headteacher was established more strongly as a result.

The Scottish Qualification for Headship

Paralleling interest and spending on various management training initiatives in schools, national government's interest in developing the management skills found across all enterprises and organisations within the UK led to the Management Charter Initiative (MCI, 1991). Within this development, which aimed to set clear and progressive standards for performance in core managerial functions, management activity was to be analysed into areas of competent performance, with corresponding describable behaviours that could be evidenced.

There was frustration among some employers and politicians that successive expensive management training programmes, even those designed with interactive activity-based features such as the MTHT modules, had not changed the management practices of heads. Policy failures were seen as at least in part a consequence of headteachers' resistance to, or failure to implement, the policies. This was the case for example in relation to the patchy implementation of '5–14', Scotland's equivalent of the English national curriculum (Malcolm and Schlapp, 1997). Interestingly, and belatedly, some of the Scottish policy community are now accepting responsibility for these and similar failures (Henderson, 2002). Under the old Scottish model, the policy itself could not be flawed, since the difficulties were attributable to implementation and ineffective management. Such a model ignores a key dimension of the management of change literature which highlights that the implementation of complex change in schools requires careful planning and realistic time scales. This 'deficit' view of the practice of school leadership was paralleled by a growing understanding, summarised in the seminal work of Eraut (1994), that professional development and learning is complex, and requires a guided and structured interaction between critical reflection and practice.

The new Labour government of the late 1990s throughout the United Kingdom made clear the importance it attached to raising the standards of schooling. After the devolution settlement for Scotland, the new Executive endorsed the declared educational priority of raising educational standards, which

> will require the highest qualities of leadership and management at all levels in schools but particularly at the top where the driving force for improvement must originate. Much is dependent on the skills and abilities of our headteachers and we owe it to them to ensure that they are fully trained and developed for the demanding tasks they face. (SOEID, 1997)

In response to an election manifesto commitment to develop a Scottish Qualification for Headship, a decision was taken to consult widely on the development of a related professional standard (SOEID, 1997). Many headteachers and school senior managers had taken MTHT modules and while some had been accredited to an extent, no coherent qualification existed and it was believed that a national framework might offer advantages and provide incentive. Additionally, the education authorities arrangements had changed, with the reversion to smaller unitary authorities in the reorganisation of 1996. Issues of scale and capacity came together with changes in the role of heads occasioned by school development planning, devolved school management and quality assurance initiatives which brought heads greater responsibilities and demanded enhanced leadership.

HMI reports on 'Standards and Quality in Scottish Schools' suggested that leadership in the great majority of primary and secondary schools was good or very good, but in about 20 per cent of schools areas of weakness in leadership existed and in about 5 per cent of schools leadership was considered unsatisfactory. The Executive's policy was to ensure that headteachers in Scottish schools had proper qualifications and training for the post of headteacher. Research was commissioned to explore the functional management competences required of new headteachers. The work done by MCI influenced developments for school leadership and management training (Casteel *et al.*, 1997; Reeves *et al.*, 1998) is evidenced in the Standard for Headship in Scotland (SOEID, 1998b, p. 6). The framework for education management agreed in Scotland was to be based on four key management functions:

- policy and planning (which includes developing partnerships with pupils, parents, the school board and the local community);
- teaching and learning (through establishing effective structures, ethos and context);
- managing people (with the stress on leadership and teamwork); and
- managing resources and finance.

In the consultation paper for the revised Standard of 2005 (SEED, 2005b) these are redefined as 'professional actions' and a fifth area added:

- leading and managing teaching and learning;
- leading and managing people;
- leading improvement;
- using resources effectively;
- building community.

When consulting on the proposed qualification for Scottish headteachers, the government (SOEID, 1997) reaffirmed the importance of leadership development:

The performance of any organisation, large or small, is crucially dependent on the quality of its leadership. Schools, be they nursery primary special or secondary, are no different from other organisations in that respect. Good headteachers can help schools rise to the challenge of curricular change and transform teaching and learning conditions whilst ineffective heads can block improvements and stifle initiative.

Defining the initial version of the Standard for Headship (SOEID, 1998b) was a collaborative process within the model of 'managed consultation' characteristic of change and development in Scottish education (Humes, 1986). Competences associated with each of the functions indicated above were 'agreed' with the profession through a consultative process in which fully drafted documents were shared with meetings of heads in different parts of the country. A development group comprising representatives from schools, education authorities, TEIs and professional associations produced a draft standard. There was further consultation at a series of meetings throughout the country. Through a process of redrafting and refinement, the initial version of the Standard for Headship (SOEID, 1998b) emerged. The Standard established as the key purpose of headship in Scotland:

> To provide the leadership and management which enables school to give every pupil high quality education and which promotes the highest possible standards of achievement.

This conflation of leadership and management is one of a number of ways in which the Standard holds in tension some of the complex issues in defining successful headship by avoiding the narrower competence-based approaches to practice, although drawing from them in a dynamic model (Figure 4.2).

Figure 4.2: SQH: Developmental themes

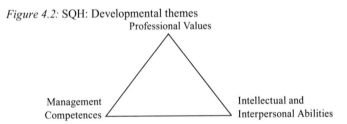

The model, which required the successful development of Professional Values, Management Competence and Intellectual and Interpersonal Abilities which operate interactively in professional practice, received considerable acclaim for its ability to hold some of these overlapping and potentially conflicting models of practice in a successful action-related tension (Kirk, 2000, pp. 57–60).

The dynamic interaction of these different elements in successful practice and situational judgement caught the open-ended, unique and unpredictable character of school leadership better than any previous statement in Scotland of the complex character of professional experience and practice. It also offered the opportunity to develop programmes of professional learning that engaged with the wider and more complex sets of issues which our earlier chapters have identified with the experience and practice of headship in modern plural democratic societies. This dynamic quality has been retained in the revised Standard of 2005.

The resulting Scottish Qualification for Headship (SQH) (for further information cf. Centre for Educational Leadership (online)) is centred on the individual candidate's values, aptitudes and attitudes plus the knowledge and skills associated with such a senior management position (O'Brien, 2000; O'Brien and Draper, 2002; O'Brien and Murphy, 2003). There is an emphasis in the learning programme for the qualification on the practical, including an industrial experience, but this is underpinned by theoretical insights, with learning modes a mix of school-based and higher education approaches, being accredited as part of Modular Master's Schemes (Landon, 1995) or equivalent. The Scottish Executive Education Department (SEED) funded pilot and full-scale implementation of two programmes – an Accelerated Route (AR) for those who were already competent school managers and a Standard Route (SR) for those seeking further development. They were both designed to lead candidates to a level of professional practice equivalent to that described in the Standard and recognised by the award of the Scottish Qualification for Headship, awarded by the First Minister of the Scottish Executive, and recognised by HEIs as a postgraduate diploma. Between 1998 and 2000 there was a series of pilot initiatives (Morris and Reeves, 2000). Two routes were developed: a standard route, normally taking two or more years to complete in part-time mode, and an accelerated mode lasting one year for those with attested prior experience. The standard route involved four Units of study:

Figure 4.3: SQH: Standard route (adapted from Reeves *et al.*, 2001)

UNIT	MODE	ACTIVITIES
Unit 1:	4-day taught course (standard and accelerated modes).	Candidates evaluate their capabilities against the Standard and use this to plan their learning and practical projects.
Units 2 and 3:	work-based learning, 9 months each (standard modes only).	Candidates develop all the competences with support and coaching from a supporter and a tutor.
Unit 4:	6-day taught course (standard and accelerated modes). Integration of learning into a strategic framework	Further development of self-awareness in relation to leadership.

The learning programme for SQH draws on the work of Kolb (1984) and Eraut (1994). Learning has to influence practice and make a real difference in schools. Learning *what* is involved in headship, thinking about *why* heads take decisions and trying out *how to* do the core activities of headship are therefore brought together in the programme. It involves learning and assessment activities which seek to make connections between the personal and professional context of the individual, the policy context in Scotland and the conceptual and research framework written up in the international literature on school leadership and management. SQH has been a unique experiment in the teaching profession in Scotland. For the first time, a national standard was defined for a particular role within the profession and a qualification piloted and developed to enable those who wished to develop their practice to meet the Standard to do so.

Operationally, the programme works within a national template, with specified Units and associated learning outcomes. This national template frames local programmes, developed and delivered in the first instance by three approved consortia consisting of universities and partner employing education authorities working in a collaborative partnership.

Within the programme, all candidates evaluate their current practice against the Standard and identify learning needs. Learning takes place through the normal methods of academic coursework (reading, reflection, written assignments, class meetings and workshops), but just as importantly through experience. It is a central part of the programmes that candidates should not just know about leadership and management but should be able to practise successfully in a contemporary school setting. To this end, work-based learning is supported by the compilation of a portfolio of evidence, assessed as a written document, but also through a field visit. Within the portfolio candidates must demonstrate that their leadership has made a difference to the learning lives of pupils through successful management practice with and through staff. Workplace learning is supported by the local authority employer and by the school headteacher (who acts as the candidate's supporter through the programme) in partnership with HEIs. Quality was assured by the national programme descriptor, nationally set performance criteria, national training within the pilot phase, and university quality assurance procedure and GTCS accreditation arrangements. There has been limited experimentation with using online learning support.

Access to the programme is controlled by local authority employers and HEIs. Equity of access, workload requirements and the status of the qualification (mandatory, desirable or optional) have been the key concerns of professional associations. The partnership model for planning and delivery ensures dialogue and mutual consideration of the operational priorities of the employer and the academic concerns of university staff. Delivery of SQH to meet these expectations gives rise to significant logistical challenges. These include: the complexity of communication across a range of stakeholders and agencies; the training of university and local authority staff involved in delivery, support and assessment; ensuring even standards of support and delivery; integrating SQH into a local staff development strategy at authority level; ensuring appropriate selection and candidacy; the burdens within school of work-based learning approaches (e.g. support and mentoring in-school); time and priority management for SQH candidates, who have heavy operational responsibilities; and maintaining national standards within a devolved delivery framework.

It also has also raised significant strategic issues connected with the planning and development of staff development strategy and models within local authorities; the planning and delivery of 'pre-SQH' management and leadership training; models of management, support and coordination at local level; and methods of developing and maintaining good partnerships between education authorities, HEIs and government.

A number of studies (O'Brien and Draper, 2001; Reeves *et al.*, 2001, Murphy *et al.*, 2002a) reviewing aspects of the programme were published in the first few years of the new qualification. A number of strengths and areas for development were suggested by such studies. Strengths of the SQH to date have included the success of the work-based learning model in influencing the practice of the learner, his or her school community, and the role of the field assessor; the power of ongoing interactive critical activity and professional practice; the balancing partnership between employers (interested in effective delivery) and HEIs (interested in ensuring that professional development does not become unreflective training and in developing a wider research base of knowledge calibrated against international best practice and literature).

However, for the next stage of development, there were several factors which needed to be considered.

- There are extensive workload pressures on candidates already in very difficult jobs and typically facing the pressures of modern private and domestic life for 30- and 40- year-olds.
- The current assessment arrangements break up the holistic character of management activity into segments. This works for descriptive and analytical purposes, but not for assessment, which can become over cumbersome and bureaucratic.
- The performance studied is related to successful leadership and management practice in a specific school context. Where an excellent school ethos, and a sense of teamwork, has already been established, a lacklustre candidate may still achieve well in all management activities because the school systems are very good.

- Where there is internal conflict and a lack of good systems at school level, even a very strong candidate may find it difficult to achieve the performance levels required.
- The competence framework has also been criticised. Riley (1998a, p. 150), while recognising the importance of competence, argues that 'it is passion and commitment which will keep the attention focused on young people'.

The SQH has developed since 1998 in response to revisions of the Standard for Headship and in relation to ongoing national discussions between universities and their partners. O'Brien and Torrance (2005) summarise how the SQH programme has developed in the light of evaluations and experience. In 2005, revised consortia-based programmes for the Scottish Qualification for Headship were accredited by the GTCS. The 2005 Standard for Headship promotes a model for development based on Professional Actions and their associated Essential Elements. Nationally, all the programmes leading to the SQH have developed along similar lines since 2005 given the dialogue between consortia, and typically are based on a cycle of self-evaluation, situational analysis and the conduct and review of a school improvement project. For example, the revised SQH programme at the University of Edinburgh, complies with the new National Standard and is designed to ensure competence in all aspects of the Standard. Those who gain the qualification will have demonstrated, both through critical reflection and through actions taken in workplace settings, the full range of competences of the effective headteacher. The current programme comprises five Courses (the fifth designed as a double course). On the successful completion of Courses 1, 2 & 3, participants are eligible for the University's Certificate in Educational Leadership and Management. On the successful completion of Courses 4 & 5, participants will be awarded the University's Diploma in Educational Leadership and Management as well as achieving the Scottish Qualification for Headship awarded by the Scottish Government. There is a facility for the Accreditation of Prior Experiential Learning (APL/APEL) to a maximum of 50 per cent for participants who can demonstrate appropriate levels of experience and/or competence.

The SQH programme combines theoretical and practical approaches through 'workplace learning'. There are two new noteworthy perspectives:

- It is not enough in the SQH programme to be able to assemble ideas and arguments effectively in an essay. Critical reflection must have shown results in the workplace and in personal development if it is to be credited.
- On the other hand, work activity that is not carefully considered in the light of research, that is solely about implementation and

does not require critical reflection, will not meet the requirements of SQH.

There is a strong focus on leadership in this new programme. Further details can be found at Scottish Qualification for Headship (2008), while the revised programme is outlined below:

Figure 4.4: SQH: Scottish Qualification for Headship (2008) revised programme

Course 1	Initially engages candidates in a Critical Self-Evaluation against the Standard for Headship (CSE) and the articulation of a programme for personal learning (PLP).
Course 2	Focuses on an analysis of the school, it's capacity for change and improvement and culminates in a detailed School Improvement Project plan (SIP).
Course 3	Involves the study of an aspect of leadership or management by comparing a participant's own school with another organisation, usually another public service, industrial or commercial organisation or in another sector of education.
Course 4	Entails a close analysis and evaluation of critical features of the change process in the participant's school.
Course 5	A double course taking as its focus implementation, monitoring and evaluation of the SIP, covering the Professional Actions and the Essential Elements of The Standard for Headship.

So what does the future for leadership development in Scotland hold? Is there a 'golden rule-book or recipe for effective leadership' (MacBeath and Myers, 1999, p. 67)? In December 2001, SEED declared that the Standard for Headship would become mandatory in 2005, and a review of SQH itself was announced, with a suggestion that there may be several ways to achieve the Standard. The national evaluation of SQH (Menter *et al.*, 2003; 2005) confirmed many of the points made by the range of initial studies, and provided SEED with much positive feedback on the SQH. The reporting of the evaluation, which involved a survey and several case studies, (Menter *et al.*, 2005, pp. 7–8) recognised that:

> ... the SQH development team was keen to ensure that the programme would have a strongly professional orientation, in spite of the lead organizations in its development being university departments of education.
>
> ... Not only were the development and delivery done collaboratively, the rationale for the programme was based on a strong social psychological view about adult learning. This included the beliefs, firstly, that learning about leadership and learning about institutional change necessarily went hand in hand and, secondly, that any

individual learner was developing in a social context which was fundamental to the learning process.

Reeves *et al.* (2001, p. 209) indicated:

The original design of the SQH programme was based on the notion that professionals develop their practice most effectively by maximising their experiential learning through engaging in reflective processes ... the effectiveness of any learning experience lies in its influence on the formation, or modification of concepts that guide the individual's basis for action.

The impact of SQH on individual candidates was marked. As Menter *et al.* (2005, p. 11) confirm:

SQH graduates believed they had been enabled to implement change and improve team working in their school. It was interesting to note they were less confident about the impact on the attainment of children. Those whom we interviewed felt this crucial measure could only be properly judged when a longer period of time had elapsed from completion of the programme.

They go on to conclude (p. 13) that the case study evidence suggested:

- school-based projects had a great impact on school culture;
- supporters (largely head teachers) benefited from involvement;
- teachers commented positively on curriculum development which resulted from the projects;
- education authority coordinators not only confirmed the above but in addition gave some insight to a wider benefit to the schools within the area; and
- the potential of the SQH programme is most fully realized when the candidate has adequate support both from the education authority and from within the school – not only from the head but also from the whole staff.

While in England NPQH is complemented by developments for headteachers at various stages of their career, for example, the Leadership Programme for Serving Headteachers (LPSH), no sustained national programme of this nature has emerged in Scotland. What other leadership development provision was required?

In 2004, the Ministerial CPD Strategy Group established a group (the Leadership and Management Pathway Subgroup – known as LAMPS) to review leadership and management development before and after SQH. As noted, subsequent adjustments and improvements, related to the revised Standard (2005) have led to a variety of programmes developing in each of the three national consortia, serving the East, West and North of the country.

These revised programmes built on the strengths of the initial programme identified in the report by Menter *et al.* (2003) and outlined above. However, there were still significant professional criticisms of aspects of the programme (TES, 2007) and nationally an 'alternative route' was commissioned by SEED and developed in collaboration with three local authorities (see SEED, 2006c). The development and evaluation of this alternative route, with a strong focus on 'coaching on the job', is under way at the time of publication, but we reflect on this and other developments and opportunities in the final chapter.

So far in this book we have discussed themes such as leadership in the contexts of democratic politics, the distributed character of leadership, schools as organisations, pressures on schools and schooling, pressures on headteachers and those in leadership positions and recent and current training initiatives. These considerations provide a platform for the discussion in the concluding chapter, of associated developments and consideration of the way ahead.

CHAPTER 5

NEW MODELS, NEXT STEPS?

Where is school leadership headed?

Although many of the examples and details of the foregoing discussion have centred particularly on the experience in Scotland, many of the issues raised are characteristic of school leadership in many societies. The kinds of educational experience we want for our children reflect our broader social and political values. In democratic societies, induction into the rights and responsibilities of democratic participation and consideration of what constitutes the appropriate distribution of power must inform our understanding and conceptual framing of our public services. Leadership, both as a concept and as a practice within this model, is widely distributed; and school communities and democratic systems must be open to its expression from unexpected directions, and not simply through the narrow channels of linear bureaucratic management and accountability systems, although bureaucratic organisation of schools must remain part of the picture. It is known from the current experience of those in leadership and management positions that they are challenged by the technical difficulties of increasingly complex operational management, by the professional challenges of reconceptualising schools, and by the moral complexity of developing communities of learning where competing, sometimes contradictory, values pull in different directions (Murphy, 2007). The agreement (SEED, 2001a) reached between teachers and their employers in Scotland following the McCrone Report (SEED, 2000b) offers some opportunities for the teaching profession in Scotland to engage with this challenging agenda, but it cannot be assumed that schools as currently designed can automatically be transformed, no matter how willing and able the teachers.

The exciting possibilities for further development of the leadership role in Scottish schools which is prefigured by recent developments is matched nationally by a renewed thrust towards devolved decision-making, situational community-based judgement and a commitment to widen local ownership of school priorities and aims (McConnell, 2002). Consideration of how the development of those who play leadership roles in our schools may progress cannot be separated from the wider context of how schools may change and how that fits with a vision for the future of Scottish society. Two examples of different school futures, based on different sets of values about school functions, are outlined below as an illustrative basis for considering this link. One compares present schooling to an ideal educational experience, but makes few practical suggestions on how the present system might move forward. The other envisages continuing evolutionary change, and puts purposeful school leadership at the heart of that change.

In 2000, the Scottish Council Foundation published an accessible and challenging document, *Changing Schools: Education in a Knowledge Society* (Boyle and Leicester, 2000). This report, billed as a 'basis for debate', outlined clearly what they saw as the deficiencies of the present schooling model, with its structural origins in the factory age, and offered suggestions about a new type of schooling model based on a different set of principles to those which underpin the present structure. It provides a convenient summary of much of the frustration with the limitations of schools as a mechanism for delivering and empowering education. They argued for a learner-focused, individualist system of education, characterised by:

1. respect for individual needs
2. continuous professional development of teachers
3. research-based practice
4. a culture of raised expectations
5. parent demand
6. clear national leadership
7. teacher ownership and flexibility
8. teamwork
9. sense of purpose
10. no early specialisation
11. intensive relationship building
12. blurring of boundaries between school and the world outside.

(Boyle and Leicester, 2000, p. 27)

These they see as the characteristics of the best current practice in the field of Special Educational Needs, a type of education 'where you have to fail to qualify'. They do not prescribe the school of the future, but offer a challenge to the present model based on its failure to deal successfully with the range of educational needs of a fluid, rapidly developing society. They would like to see education remodelled and schools reconstructed.

This model of change, based on aspirational visions, not practical steps, is in contrast to the vision of the future which emerged from the 'National Debate' on education in Scotland (Scottish Executive, 2003). The debate and the Executive's response (SEED, 2003a) showed that the civic community is cautious and evolutionary in its approach to educational change and respects and supports the schools and schooling models currently in place, despite their structural difficulties and tensions. This limited evolutionary model of change is also evident in the widespread commitment of funds for at least a 25-year period, through Private Public Partnership (PPP) schemes, to school buildings whose design is based on current curriculum and staffing models. This second illustrative example of speculation on next steps in schooling also envisages continuing evolutionary change.

Although these are only two of many different examples of possible futures for Scottish schools, over the next four years, the ambitious plan set out by the new Scottish Government will challenge the Scottish system to bring these two strands together in implementing the visionary 'Curriculum for Excellence' (see SEED, 2008). Can the aspirational ideal curriculum vision be made real? – that is the challenge facing Scottish state school education, and its school leaders, now. Other schools and other systems face similar wide-ranging challenges.

In many societies, including the UK, independent schools take pride in maintaining their distinctive linkage of heritage and future, and strong identity in a time of turbulent social change. In the emerging East European democracies, democratisation and economic capacity are key challenges, from a very sudden, revolutionary, starting point with the collapse of the Soviet bloc. We have already argued that in Scotland, traditional hierarchical approaches to school organisation do not sit easily with ambitions to widen civic participation and for schools to model democratic processes of community building, empowering and respecting every individual. In England, diversity in schooling, associated with specialisation or with particular faith communities, is currently seen by government as a strength (DFEE, 2001). This democratic vision seems to value freedom to choose above equality of access. Scotland has preferred, through the National Debate and subsequent strong political pronouncements (McConnell, 2002), with continuing support for this approach by the recently elected Scottish Nationalist government, to balance freedom and equality by providing a standard type of school across all communities although this standardisation may be challenged by the new approach to the curriculum in Scottish Schools – *A Curriculum for Excellence* (SEED, 2004) for which a dedicated website has been established, see A Curriculum for Excellence (online). In this vision it is likely that some social tensions, which are dispersed by choice in more open systems, will be held within the school. Such tensions will require sophisticated handling by socially and organisationally aware school leaders.

Who will our future school leaders be?

We have argued that the dispersal of leadership within democratic school communities, whether this happens through conscious redesign or through the inevitable evolution occasioned by greater plurality and empowerment, should cause us to reconceptualise leadership. More people within the school community need to be involved in preparation for wider participation in leadership. However, at the same time as we see the increasing plurality of communities and consequent complexity of the models there is a trend of fewer teachers seeking promotion to headship, the leadership role with the most potential to influence developments within a school. This trend raises the spectre of a headteacher supply problem in Scotland similar to that already identified elsewhere, for example by Williams (2001) in Ontario, Howson (2002) in England, and Barty *et al.* (2005) in Australia. Both workload and bureaucracy have been highlighted (in Chapter 3) as important factors affecting headteacher supply. Williams also identified difficulties in the relationship between local authorities and headteachers as significant.

In addition, in Scotland, headteacher supply seemed likely to be influenced by the introduction of Chartered Teacher (CT) status, following the McCrone agreement. This high status non-managerial career route may attract a number who would formerly have sought promotion. It offers a competing career route particularly in the earlier stages before headship; while the initial uptake by experienced teachers has been disappointing there are signals that those now with five years' experience as classroom teachers may embark in increasing numbers on programmes leading to CT status. However, an increase of personnel with an enhanced competence and confidence in learning and teaching strategies may result in more taking up headship. Southworth (2005, p. 75) recognises the school leader's emphasis on student learning and achievement:

> what distinguishes school leaders from leaders in other organizations is their desire and responsibility to enhance students' learning. It is precisely this focus on students' development which makes school leadership distinctive and different from many other forms of leadership. Indeed, it is this commitment to improving students' achievements which drives so many individuals to become school leaders. They explicitly seek and want to make a difference to the schools they lead.

Not only is headship changing therefore, but there remains a question about whether it is attractive enough in competition with apparently less stressful alternatives.

There are, at present, limited Scottish data on headteacher supply, although in 2008 the Scottish Government funded a research project on the 'Recruitment and Retention of Head Teachers'. This project will report in 2009, but we may infer similar patterns to those in other developed state education systems. Suffering from innovation overload, squeezed between the centralising rigour of a strong national framing of school education in terms of accountability and an increasing openness and empowerment of those within school communities, headteachers may see themselves as political 'plate spinners', balancing different forces within the school, rather than as educational leaders, able to develop creative local models. Thomson *et al.* (2003a;, p. 128) in their analysis of American media accounts found two contrasting images of school leadership: namely, 'overworked, underpaid and undervalued victim principal' or alternatively the 'saviour principal ... who is able to create happy teams of teachers, students and parents for whom all reform is possible'.

Such tensions may be particularly experienced by the many headteachers currently in post who have received little or no leadership preparation, although in recent years this has been improving across the country through the induction and coaching and mentoring initiatives discussed below. The concepts and ideas advanced in this and similar books provide interpretation and explanation of some of the pressures and forces which act on the headteacher. Explanation and understanding can help to restore the sense of professional control which those who fulfil these demanding roles require if they are to be leaders and not jugglers. High-quality preparation for the unpredictable complexities of headship has never been more important.

Factors in the preparation of school leadership

The argument so far has established that the type of school is closely related to the type of leadership required. However, even if we were looking ahead at a clear linear model of school development – one where plans led to the changes intended, where political direction was uncontested, where civic, religious, professional and personal values were aligned, where social and economic change could be reliably predicted – there would still be other influences to be considered. These involve consideration of effectiveness in adult and professional learning, related issues arising from current structures of professional development and progression, and concerns arising from studying existing practice in school leadership. Each of these areas is now briefly considered.

In relation to models of professional learning, Chapter 4 has already outlined how understandings of the complex linkage of motivation and purpose, experiential learning and reflective practice have impacted on the design of increasingly sophisticated programmes of professional development such as the Scottish Qualification for Headship. Moreover, if learning is to interact meaningfully with practice within professional communities of practice, then it cannot any longer be constructed only, or even primarily, as an individual experience. Programmes such as SQH, with their strong emphasis on developing and improving practice through self-evaluative ownership of the learning, succeed best in a school context where the pre-existing school culture is already in tune with the improvement model espoused. Significant problems can be caused for the learners in work-based learning programmes in which the learner is isolated within a school culture which does not support the improvement proposed (Reeves *et al.*, 2002). In addition, Cowie (2005, p. 396) confirming earlier work (Murphy *et al.*, 2002) suggests that:

> although the work-based action learning model underpinning the SQH is powerful and effective, successful completion of the programme appears to be heavily influenced by the school context and the supportive environment provided by the EA [education authority].

Restructuring of the profession can have an influence beyond credentials. In Scotland, the agreement (SEED, 2001a) on teachers' conditions of service and contracts has made it a requirement of registration that teachers undertake 35 hours per year of professional development, negotiated with their headteacher or supervisor, and designed to balance and update their skills. This requirement gives new opportunities to teachers to consider leadership at all levels within a school community and to reassess their practice in the light of other models. In 2001, the National College for School Leadership (see online) developed a five-stage framework to describe progression in leadership throughout and within a professional career. In Scotland the Leadership and Management sub-group devised a similar framework (SEED, 2003b). The national CPD framework for education leaders in schools and education authorities attempts to define the relationship between leader and manager (p. 4):

> A leader secures the support, commitment and enthusiasm of staff and so enables the smooth and effective running of often-complex systems of management. Leadership is about defining what the future should look like, agreeing a shared vision and inspiring others to make it happen, even in the face of adversity.

Management, however, might more appropriately be viewed as the practical application of leadership skills. Effective leadership provides positive direction and purpose. Effective management ensures that purpose can be achieved.

The framework has four broad levels, through which progression takes place:

- **Project** leadership (time-limited, small-scale projects for teachers early in their career);
- **Team** leadership (regular leadership of working groups or of established teams of staff);
- **School** leadership (including the Scottish Qualification for Headship);

- **Strategic** leadership (for those with overall responsibility for a school, or engaged in leading major initiatives at a local or national level).

Several education authorities and other CPD providers have subsequently aligned their provision with this framework. Such frameworks can offer a useful template within which to situate desirable career development at different stages, but should not be used to limit and constrain development.

Whatever professional preparation programmes are available, much ongoing learning and development will continue to be based in the co-construction of meaning and quality which takes place within individual school communities. Learning here takes place through the collaborative peer relationships involved in teamwork, in mentoring and being mentored, in supervised task completion and in developing collective responses to new requirements and newly prioritised needs of the school or its staff. Structures of professional development and progression can in this context both promote and inhibit development. Much of the Teachers' Agreement in Scotland (SEED, 2001a) was seen by employers as concerned with introducing flexibility into the teachers' contract to allow creative local discussion and agreement on widening the responsibilities and associated development of all teachers, not just those with designated managerial responsibilities (Thorburn, 2002). More collegial decision-making within schools, and wider responsibilities beyond curriculum for teachers, will in this view both require and encourage professional development. This change of course has further implications for the development of those who will lead this process at school level. In more clearly directed systems for professional development, understanding of leadership and democracy should feature. However, we have already recorded our view of the initial anomalous situation in Scotland where the new agreement both required the greater collegial involvement of teachers in leadership activities and the omission of any kind of leadership preparation from the programmes of professional development leading to Chartered Teacher. This situation has developed further more recently. Major contributions are often expected of CTs, and while there is continuing recognition that CTs have no management role (National CPD Team, 2005a) there is every expectation that CTs will make a major contribution to schools and in so doing exercise leadership as illustrated in Appendix 2 of the paper by:

- leading and/or contributing to small-scale project either within school or across cluster with support of member of senior leadership team; carrying out appropriate professional actions, reflecting upon experience of leading, and completing project and evaluating what has been achieved;

- supporting/coaching/mentoring colleagues, including students and probationer teachers.

So there is some evidence of teachers outside or not yet part of management structures having opportunities to exercise leadership and to contribute to wider professional obligations. This is further reinforced in Scotland by recent developments in the Inspection process (HMIE, 2007a) which expect distributed forms of leadership to be in evidence in schools and describe good practice in leadership through four different quality indicators.

Another worthwhile perspective on professional development has already been highlighted by the report of various empirical studies (in Chapter 3) into headship preparation and the concerns of those in post about the 'surprises' which awaited them. These studies carry implications for the initial and ongoing support of those newly appointed to positions with substantial leadership responsibility. The complex and unpredictable character of the challenges involved in leadership in school communities in the twenty-first century requires that they have access to a wide range of conceptual resources, moral and ethical understanding and social awareness. These understandings cannot be dropped into 'empty vessels'. They develop through opportunities to construct and test out the meaning of individual situations and challenges, in collaboration with others. Whatever the 'stage' of career development, everyone who participates in leadership activities within the school can benefit from access to a variety of professional development activities that help to structure and to interpret the complex events and interactions of the school community. These interactions and events are not simply concerned with technical aspects of pedagogy, important as these are to the school. In analysing school communities and the leadership they require, we saw that leadership roles engage with aesthetic and imaginative aspects of communities, with operational and bureaucratic requirements and safety-nets, with social entrepreneurship, with political awareness and the development of democratic inclusion, and lastly with moral stewardship. The menu of development opportunities required to support this kind of engagement is well beyond the narrow technicist models of management training favoured in some quarters in previous decades, but promises to engage with the breadth of experiences and challenges of leadership in contemporary school communities.

The challenge remains for employers, professional associations, universities and others to develop that wide menu, so that skills of situational judgement and pedagogical excellence, joined with broad social vision and ethical understanding, can be developed in professionally relevant settings to support those in leadership roles. This will require a new knowledge base – a new map of professional practice, more situationally sensitive and detailed than our present broad-brush prescriptions. It is suggested this will involve: experimentation into different models of professional development, rigorously evaluated; sharing of practice through research publication; dialogue; a more developed conceptualisation of what democratic leadership involves; a wide range of development activities, accessed through individually supported self-evaluation, including the short and long term, team and individual, conceptual challenge and experiential development and involving rigour through triangulated assessment of progression. In Scotland, as elsewhere, these challenges will only be met if the development of leadership within our schools is taken seriously and researched and resourced effectively. What has been done to date to meet such challenges?

Shaping the programmes

Our developing understanding of schools, of leadership, of the experience of those in leadership roles and of the kinds of professional development that can support and improve practice leads us to a more complex and sophisticated framing of leadership activities and of the range of development activities needed to support quality in leadership. A different set of issues is involved in the development and support of leadership, broadly conceived, from those involved in the support of management.

Those in leadership positions need to have access to a wide range of resources, skills and abilities, and to be able to apply these both strategically, in terms of the long-term direction of the school, and operationally in the complex situations, involving individual people, which occur within school communities. They will draw on cognitive resources, which allow them to understand and interpret pedagogical practice and democratic social process. They will need affective resources, developed and stored within themselves, which support their emotional work with and for others. They will need access to the spiritual and moral resources that allow them to explore with others in their school communities the values and purposes of education, issues of social justice and the ethics of the school community. Such cognitive, affective and moral resources, informed by experience and situational knowledge, offer the best guarantees of good judgement in dealing with the tensions and dilemmas of schooling. It is not just headteachers, and others in positions of authority within and outwith schools, who are called to develop these resources, but all who share in leadership activity.

For management, a more restricted, but more focused set, of skills and abilities is required. The earlier discussion in Chapter 4 established some of that difference. Effective managers are concerned with implementation and efficiency, with systems, grounded in best practice, with developing and supporting teams, with clear communication and presentation, with using technology wisely and creating the safe infrastructure within which the day-to-day work of the school can be conducted. These tasks are more clearly related to job function within the hierarchy of school staffing.

In the description of good practice expressed in the current Scottish Standard for Headship (SEED, 2005c), leadership and management activities mix easily, as they do in reality. In the light of the more flexible models of school organisation currently being promoted in Scotland, it may prove helpful when reconceptualising school leadership for the next more uncertain phase of school development. The revision of the Standard failed to make clear what belongs mainly in the field of leadership, that is, a set of desirable characteristics for any and all of those who live and work in school communities; and what belongs mainly to management, and is consequently more closely associated with particular roles and stages of career.

To support the acquisition of this varied set of understandings, broad leadership abilities and more focused management skills, a broad and balanced menu of development and support opportunities will be required. In a teaching profession used to twenty years of 'empty vessel' staff development, the more empowering model envisaged by the McCrone Report will require re-culturing. The maintenance of records of professional development, the wider use of portfolios to retain evidence and acquire credit for development and the associated streamlined process of annual professional development review, offer a new structure. Within this structure, regular self-assessment against agreed targets, national standards and quality benchmarks will allow a balancing of the 'top–down' requirements of the employer and the aspirations of the teacher. It is unlikely that a one-year cycle will offer either the structure or the breadth which this new climate demands. Teachers might be better to plan, in broad-brush terms, over a five-year cycle, to ensure the right kinds of balance in what they choose from the menu of possible development opportunities.

Framing choice to ensure balance over the medium term is the key to successful programmes. A menu from which balanced programmes could be constructed would include different types of learning – through task planning and implementation, through peer team activity, through visiting or viewing or observing, through challenging thinking and discussion, and through externally assessed activity. Any one of these on its own will not provide the range and choice needed to respond in a balanced way to the situational needs of individual teachers. Balance will also need to be sought in relation to content – understanding or competent skill development, strategic involvement or operational effectiveness, social or pedagogical.

A further balance to be maintained across the medium term is between the needs of the school community and the needs of the individual. Individual needs are likely to be, at least in part, conditioned by issues of career and current responsibility. Acting headteachers, longstanding deputes who do not wish to be heads, aspiring young teachers who wish to develop as fast as they can on all fronts, experienced headteachers who have reached their first plateau of achievement, these and other groups will have quite specific needs related to their current role, as well as the more generalised and recurring issues of practice.

Beyond the content of the menu of development opportunities from which staff should be encouraged to choose if they are to maintain a balanced medium-term profile to their development and support experiences, diversity will also strengthen the mechanisms for delivery. There should be opportunities to undertake such development work in holiday periods, on Saturday mornings, online, through the use of in-house mentoring, and in work-based learning. Of course we recognise that work–life balance arguments need to be considered. For example, CPD for the job is part of the job but heads and others in responsible positions need to protect places for growth and renewal that are away from the job. Accredited programmes should be available, but also non-accredited. Some will be short half-day 'top-ups' in key management areas, some longitudinal development with a peer group aimed at the deeper roots of professional practice, such as SQH. Team development opportunities should sit alongside individual opportunities, especially if leadership is a shared activity.

This is the ideal. Those undertaking leadership roles are informed and self-aware. They have access to the conceptual and best practice resources through publication and knowledge sharing so that they can construct and choose a balanced medium-term programme to support their own improvements in practice. This choice would be based on a menu of development and support activities which keep them fresh, help them to deal with the challenges and tensions of leadership activity, offer specific development in relation to their changing managerial functions, and build the base of their successful practice.

There have been developments in encouraging the use of ICT and online communities (see Online Communities, 2008) such as *Heads Together* of which the evaluation of the pilot project (Granville, 2003) indicated that 'despite relatively low levels of access and usage, headteachers are broadly positive'. More recently this concept has been extended to Depute Heads (Blane, 2007).

The publication of *Ambitious, Excellent Schools: Our Agenda for Action* in 2004 established a new agenda with respect to school leadership. Several commitments were identified:

- establish a leadership academy, by the end of 2005, to give access to world-class thinking on school leadership and to allow the sharing of experience of school leaders;
- revise the Standard for Headship in 2005 to ensure it continues to reflect shared leadership priorities in education;
- establish new routes to achieve the Standard for Headship, during 2006, to provide choice and alternatives to the Scottish Qualification for Headship; and

- recommend new and more rigorous procedures for selecting headteachers to take effect from the end of 2005.

As a result, the Leadership Sub-group of the Continuous Professional Development Advisory Group (subsequently described as the Leadership Strategy Group) was charged with:

- redefining the Standard for Headship;
- developing alternative routes to achieving the Standard;
- considering headteacher appointment processes and making recommendations; and
- supporting development of the Leadership Academy.

Has this agenda been overtaken successfully? What progress has been made to date?

In a discussion document (*Ambitious, Excellent Schools: Leadership – A Discussion Paper*, SEED, 2005a), SEED claimed that the original Standard for Headship, published in 1998, and the related development of the Scottish Qualification for Headship, detailed in Chapter 4, had made a significant contribution to improving the quality of leadership in Scottish schools. Certainly the independent national evaluation of SQH (Menter *et al.*, 2003; 2005) supported this conclusion. The publication of 'Ambitious, excellent schools' affirmed SEED's commitment to Leadership in schools and the opportunity to update the then Standard for Headship, something which had been promised some time before was overtaken rapidly and the new Standard quickly followed after the consultation. By and large there was agreement about the broad sweep of the new Standard (SEED, 2005c), although there were regrets that a standard for Leadership was not being mooted to recognise the growing awareness that headteachers were a very important part of the leadership jigsaw but not the only one, especially in terms of succession planning and in relation to concerns about recruitment and retention of headteachers. Perhaps an opportunity was lost to lay down a marker at this point and to provide an impetus to creating larger reservoirs of emerging talent subsequently willing to take on specific roles? This was one of the declared priority areas:

- increasing the mentoring and coaching capacity in Scottish education;
- designing and developing flexible approaches to meeting the Standard for Headship;
- accessing and sharing best practice from Scotland, the rest of the UK and beyond;
- supporting the development of leadership capacity at all levels of the education system;

- establishing additional support and development mechanisms for headteachers who are new in post;
- supporting local authorities in leadership succession planning.

Many of these suggestions mirror our earlier discussion above regarding a wide range of resources, approaches and provision for CPD. SEED established a broad-based initiative with all 32 local authorities to develop coaching and mentoring skills and, importantly, capacity. Up to £50,000 was provided to each authority to implement a focused coaching/mentoring project. Several education authorities used this to promote coaching and mentoring as approaches to professional development and induction for new and existing headteachers (see CPD Scotland, 2008). For example, the Moray Council Coaching for Change Project: Good practice extract from HMIE report: The Moray Council (HMIE, 2008b). The confidence expressed in the efficacy of coaching approaches might be fairly criticised, since to date there is minimal research evidence that coaching will really be the 'tipping point' in the continuing search for the optimum approach to CPD.

Certainly coaching offers much potential, but one would have to assume that the traditional hierarchical model of Scottish education had disappeared entirely to have confidence that coaching was anything other than part of the solution and then possibly only when a large cadre of qualified and skilled coaches emerge. Coaching is an approach which should be included in a range of available provision lest it only reify existing practice.

What did cause excitement was the proposal for alternative routes to meeting the Standard for Headship (SfH). SEED had declared that all newly appointed head teachers would be expected to meet the SfH after August 2005. While the Scottish Qualification for Headship was endorsed by SEED as valuable development experience for many aspirant headteachers, their view was influenced by the National CPD Team's data gathered from focus groups, local authority and school visits and one-to-one discussions. This data suggested a need for alternative forms of development activity, which met different personal and professional needs and yet encouraged all those with the potential to undertake the post of headteacher to pursue the Standard for Headship. Greater flexibility was called for amid concerns that the then three SQH consortia could never produce enough qualified candidates to meet potential demand. Additionally, in *Ambitious, Excellent Schools*, the Minister had made a commitment to providing choice and flexibility for aspirant headteachers, by enabling them to identify their own needs and to pursue personalised development pathways. The consultation (SEED, 2006c) on flexible routes involved a discussion paper and associated focus groups. It was recognised that any flexible route would need to be both adaptable to individual needs and be rigorous in assessment for it to gain professional credibility and parity of esteem with the SQH. Consideration of the responses by key stakeholders (namely, GTCS, employers, professional associations and higher education) to this consultation reveal interesting perspectives. Few disagreed with the principle of flexibility, but there were continuing concerns about equity and rigour associated with different approaches. Formal self-evaluation by teachers prior to entry was regarded as important. There were concerns about capacity of schools and education authorities to support developments of this nature. All stakeholders viewed as critical the need to ensure assessors and coaches were fully trained, as was the continuing involvement of higher education in the process of determining if a candidate had achieved the Standard. Universities indicated their concerns about lack of data and analysis generally in the school leadership and management arena which would permit informed decision-making, and suggested that the proposal replicated certain SQH structures and speculated about the economies of such an approach. Indeed it was suggested that specific proposals associated with making the SQH programme more flexible and responsive – already shared by certain universities with SEED – provided much more flexibility. The universities indicated the proposals strongly resembled the former SQH *accelerated route* which had been discontinued because government felt the pool of experienced personnel had been used up. Higher education also reiterated their concerns about quality assurance across a range of flexible options and comparability with the SQH. Not surprisingly from education authorities there were concerns about viability, especially for the continuance of the SQH as employers had invested significantly in partnerships with universities in the design and delivery of SQH (Murphy *et al.*, 2002a; 2002b). Employers also recognised that not all schools would be able to provide good development opportunities and that there were capacity and funding issues. The teacher unions wanted wider provision for leadership at various levels and fairness in any approach to succession planning, and like other stakeholders saw the GTCS as a possible location for the governance of any scheme or programme which might emerge as the SfH uniquely among Scottish teacher standards remains under government control.

The government in the light of such a response, and presumably heartened by the acceptance of the notion of flexibility, outlined their view (SEED, 2006b) and determined that a pilot project of a coaching reliant alternative to SQH be progressed. The principal reasons for offering a new alternative route were outlined as:

- the 'individual lifestyles and professional commitments' of teachers required consideration;
- individual approaches to learning should be recognised in CPD provision;
- a continuing concern that the number of SQH candidates not

completing would exacerbate unfilled head teacher vacancies and an attractive flexible alternative might deal with this;
* the belief that such an alternative would prove cost neutral and that alternatives could happily co-exist with SQH provision accessing the funding provided by SEED to education authorities.

Three education authorities were funded to take 10 candidates each through this flexible route and an independent evaluation is expected in late 2008. Flexible routes had become a pilot of an alternative route, the structure of which was briefly sketched out without significant rationale in the SEED document (2006b), and indicated that assessment should broadly emulate elements contained in the existing SQH. Coaching and intervention was to relate to personal and professional action plans aligned to the SfH. Anecdotal evidence suggests that in the process of the pilot, the coaching emphasis adopted has focused on interpersonal skills and personal transformation – worthy in themselves but not necessarily guaranteeing the development of competent managers and leaders. Whatever the outcome of the evaluation of this alternative route, it should be hoped that other alternatives yet to emerge are not precluded. One might conjecture about the use of the term 'flexible' itself, perhaps it would be more honest to describe it as an alternative route because the structure proposed continues to have hugely inflexible elements in it. The university sector made representations about testing the flexibility of SQH in similar manner and government accepted a tender from the Centre for Educational Leadership in the University of Edinburgh. The University's flexible alternative to SQH (while embedding significant taught elements of the existing programme) has focused also on individual coaching/tutoring – an evaluation is also expected later in 2008. There has also been pilot experimentation in the Western consortium to test a flexible coaching and mentoring route. What may emerge from this and the Edinburgh pilot experience is an umbrella of different types of provision retaining flexibility, respecting individuality, continuing practical grounded experiences combined with reflection, maintaining rigour with exposure to current research and knowledge about leadership and management, and providing a well understood, and so far supported by employers, quality assured learning, development and assessment process.

Headteacher appointment procedures were quickly dealt with by the National CPD Team (2005b) based on consultation with education authorities that contributed to a new Statutory Instrument (SEED, 2007).

However there was neither enthusiasm, nor resourcing, for a bricks-and-mortar Leadership Academy in Scotland, along the lines of NCSL. Instead of a place, the 'academy' prefigured in the 'Ambitious, Excellent Schools' proposals was conceived as an agenda for change and development. This leadership 'agenda' has been altogether more difficult to tie down. Currently,

Learning and Teaching Scotland (LTS) has responsibility for progressing the leadership agenda taking over from the Leadership Strategy group, but there appears to be a lack of national guidance and thrust – much is being done by LTS and other stakeholders pursuing various projects, for example SEED-funded visits by international thought leaders to Scotland, trips by selected Scottish educational leaders to the leadership summer school at Harvard and a subsequent Scottish International Leadership Summer School, now in its second year. However, it is difficult to detect an overall strategy in this. Stakeholders such as the professional associations are now taking a keener interest, especially in CPD provision; and partnerships are emerging beyond the traditional education authority/university arrangements. Undoubtedly this will progress in years to come. Issues remain, however, not least the capacity of the Scottish systems and the 32 differently sized local authorities who run the vast majority of schools, to deliver the kinds of development agenda set by national government.

Developing capacity to deliver

In Scotland, we desperately lack capacity to deliver consistently across the country. Neither local authorities, nor universities, the two main partners in delivering SQH for example, may have the capacity on their own to develop such a wide menu of programmes, offering choice and tailored opportunities across the range of professional needs. Small authorities in particular may lack the expertise within their centre staff, and the resources to 'second in' from schools. Even large authorities struggle to provide a sufficiently wide menu to meet needs. It seems clear that government has no interest in taking over the role of providing such a menu nationally but sees itself as setting strategic direction. Following the recent parliamentary election, the new government established a Concordat with local authorities (Scottish Executive, 2007) for the delivery of local services, including education. The terms of this Concordat are such that central government will adopt even more of a 'hands off' approach in relation to local delivery, suggesting that there may develop even greater inconsistencies of provision in school leadership development, at a time when – we have argued above – the devolution of responsibility on curriculum argues for enhanced local leadership skills.

In this situation the development of strategic partnerships between employers, professional bodies and universities is essential. Each of these partners brings to the table a unique and worthwhile contribution. Employers have an obligation to hold their teachers accountable for the quality of their work; they also typically have strengths in well-developed programmes in key areas of development and support such as induction. Professional associations bring a practice-based understanding of the current issues and concerns. Their support networks, strategic grasp and independent standpoint provide a useful counterweight to the power of the employer in determining how and why development will take place. Universities bring a critical edge to the table. They have access to best practice internationally. They can frame what appears to be reactive situationally bound experience within highly organised disciplinary structures, offering a different way of making sense of the situation beyond the experience of those who are in it. They bring discipline to the processes of evaluation, with their legitimate and rigorous concern for reliability and validity and their traditions of peer scrutiny of findings and methods. They have a tradition of publication of evidence, sharing knowledge in highly structured ways.

Although SQH has offered some experience of such partnership, there are obstacles to development. In the absence of such partnerships in the past, the Scottish teaching profession has lacked the high quality research base of its own practice with which it could engage. Much of the research literature used to support reflection on the current approach to school leadership is English, Canadian, American and Australian. The OECD Report (2007) illustrates the dearth of published Scottish material because, at least in part, there has been limited linkage between academic understanding and professional practice. More research activity is needed, to support the quantum leap in leadership development envisaged by the wide ranging sets of issues identified above. Although there has been substantial additional money provided by government to support CPD for teachers, the wide range of leadership development needs identified above will not be met without continuing resourcing. It is therefore worrying that the recent Concordat between education authorities and central government to prevent ring-fencing of funding makes teacher CPD an easy target for budget cuts.

However, there is much to be hopeful about. We have dipped our toes in the water with SQH, and the attempts to create more flexibility may bear fruit. Some authorities (such as the five central Scotland authorities) have already pooled resources to support management and leadership development at various stages. Strong education authority/university partnerships exist in the South East and Western consortias. Glasgow and Edinburgh education authorities have established provision in relation to CPD for project management while Highland is pursuing online provision. 'A Curriculum for Excellence' undoubtedly provides many opportunities for a range of teachers to take leadership initiatives. The Centre for Educational Leadership at the University of Edinburgh continues its mission to develop capacity to support leadership support and development in Scottish schools. The Virtual Staff College promotes leadership development and capacity among education authority officers. In many other parts of the country, collaborative partnerships are putting in place some of the building blocks of effective programmes, programmes which offer choice, balance and excitement, and programmes which aim to give access to the range of issues which those involved in school leadership will need if they are to set a good course for and with their school communities over the next ten or twenty years. We must now take responsibility for building more coherence, structure, choice and differentiation into these programmes. This is the central challenge if we are to build the kind of leadership capacity which schools increasingly demand.

REFERENCES

ACAS (2006) *Health and Employment*, London: ACAS

Allix, N. and Gronn, P. (2005) ' "Leadership" as a Manifestation of Knowledge', *Educational Management, Administration & Leadership*, Vol. 33, No. 2, pp. 181–96

Australian Secondary Principals Association, Australian Heads of Independent Schools Association and Catholic Secondary Principals Association (ASPA, AHISA, CaSPA) (2003) *The Best Job in the World with some of the Worst Days Imaginable*, self-published

Ball, S. (1987) *The Micropolitics of the School*, London: Methuen

Barber, B. (1994) *An Aristocracy of Everyone*, New York: Oxford University Press

Barty, K., Thomson, P., Blackmore, J., and Sachs, J. (2005) 'Unpacking the issues: researching the shortage of school principals in two states in Australia', *The Australian Educational Researcher*, Vol. 32, No. 3, pp. 1–18

Beatty, B. (2000) *The Paradox of the Emotion and Educational Leadership*, Bristol: The British Educational Management Association

Begley, P. (2004) 'Understanding valuation processes: exploring the linkage between motivation and action', in Begley, P. (ed.) (2004) Special Issue on 'Understanding and Responding Ethically to the Dilemmas of School Based Leadership', *International Studies in Educational Administration* vol. 32, no. 2, pp. 4–17

Bennett, N., Wise, C., Woods, P. and Harvey, J. A. (2003) *Distributed Leadership*, Nottingham: National College for School Leadership

Bennis, W. G. and Nanus, B. (1985) *Leaders: The Strategy for Taking Charge*, New York: Harper and Row

Blane, D. (2007) Deputes put heads together, *Times Educational Supplement*, 17 August (online). Available from URL: www.tes.co.uk/search/story/?story_id=2421712 (accessed 1 August 2008)

Bloomer, K. (2003) 'The local governance of education: a political perspective', in Bryce, T. and Humes, W. (eds) (2003) *Scottish Education*, second edn, Edinburgh: Edinburgh University Press. pp. 159–67

Boyle, M. and Leicester, G. (2000) *Changing Schools: Education in a Knowledge Society*, Edinburgh: The Scottish Council Foundation

Brundrett, M. (2001) 'The development of school leadership preparation programmes in England and the USA: a comparative analysis', *Educational Management & Administration*, Vol. 29, No. 2, pp. 229–45

Bush, T. (1998) 'NPQH: the key to effective school leadership', *School Leadership and Management*, Vol. 18, No. 3, pp. 321–33

Calabrese, R. and Zepeda, S. J. (1999) 'Decision-making: an alternative approach in the development of principals', *The International Journal of School Management*, Vol. 13, pp. 6–13

Caldwell, B. and Spinks, J. (1995) *Leading the Self Managing School*, London: Falmer Press

Carlyle, T. (1841) *On Heroes, Hero-Worship, and the Heroic in History*

Carr, D. (2000) *Professionalism and Ethics in Teaching*, London: Routledge

Carr, D. and Landon, J. (1998) 'Teachers and schools as agencies of values education: reflections on teachers' perceptions Part I: the role of the teacher', *The Journal of Beliefs and Values*, Vol. 19, No. 2, pp. 165–76

Carr, D. and Landon, J. (1999) 'Teachers and schools as agencies of values education: reflections on teachers' perceptions Part II: the hidden curriculum', *The Journal of Beliefs and Values*, Vol. 20, No. 1, pp. 21–9

Carr, W. and Hartnett, A. (1996) *Education and the Struggle for Democracy*, Buckingham: Open University Press

Casteel, V., Forde, C., Reeves, J. and Lynas, R. (1997) *A Framework for Leadership and Management Development in Scottish Schools*. Glasgow: QIE, University of Strathclyde

Centre for Educational Leadership, Moray House, www.cel.ed.ac.uk (accessed 1 August 2008)

Chakrabarti, M. and Cadman, M. (2003) 'Social Work Services' in Bryce, T. and Humes, W. (eds) (2003) *Scottish Education*, second edn, Edinburgh: Edinburgh University Press, pp. 853–64

Copley, T. (2002) 'Thomas Arnold: lessons for today', *Times Educational Supplement*, London, 22 February

Cowie, M. (2001) *Talking Heads*, Aberdeen Centre for Educational Research, Aberdeen: University of Aberdeen

Cowie, M. (2005) 'A silver lining with a grey cloud? the perspective of unsuccessful participants in the Scottish Qualification for Headship Programme across the North of Scotland', *Journal of In-service Education*, Vol. 31, No. 2, pp. 393–410

CPD Scotland (2008) 'Coaching and mentoring' (online). Available from URL: www.ltscotland.org.uk/cpdscotland/cpdconfer/coachingandmentoring/coachingl/index.asp (accessed 1 August 2008)

Cranston, N, Ehrich, L. and Billot, J. (2003) 'The secondary school principalship in Australia and New Zealand: an investigation of changing roles', *Leadership and Policy in Schools*, Vol. 2, No. 3, pp. 159–88

Cuban, L. (1996) 'Reforming the practice of educational administration through managing dilemmas', in Jacobson, S., Hickcox, E. and Stevenson, R. (eds) (1996) *School Administration: Persistent Dilemmas in Preparation and Practice*, Westport, CN: Praeger, pp. 3–17

Curriculum for Excellence, www.ltscotland.org.uk/curriculumforexcellence/ (accessed 1 August 2008)

Dadds, M. (1997) 'Continuing professional development: nurturing the expert within', *British Journal of In-service Education*, Vol. 23, No. 1, pp. 31–8

Dalin, P. (1998) *School Development: Theories and Strategies*, London: Cassell

Day, C., Harris, A. and Hadfield, M. (2001) 'Grounding knowledge of schools in stakeholder realities: a multi-perspective study of effective school leaders', *School Leadership and Management*, Vol. 21, No. 1, pp. 19–42

Day, C., Harris, A., Hadfield, M., Tolley, H., and Beresford, J. (2000) *Leading Schools in Times of Change*, Buckingham: Open University Press

DES (1959) *Primary Education*, London: HMSO

DES (1977) *Ten Good Schools*, London: Department of Education and Science

Dempster, N. and Logan, L. (1998) 'Expectations of school leaders: an Australian picture', in MacBeath, J. (ed.) (1998) *Effective School Leadership: Responding to Change*, London: Paul Chapman, pp. 80–97

Dempster, N. and Mahoney, P. (1998) 'Ethical challenges in school leadership', in MacBeath, J. (ed.) (1998) *Effective School Leadership: Responding to Change*, London: Paul Chapman, pp. 125–39

Dempster, N. and Berry, V. (2003) 'Blindfolded in a minefield: principals' ethical decision making', *Cambridge Journal of Education*, Vol. 33, No. 3, pp. 457–77

DFEE (2001) *Schools, Building on Success*, Norwich: The Stationery Office

Draper, J., Kidd, J., Knowles, I. and Turner, D. (1995) *Evaluation of Headteacher Management Training*, research·report for Lothian Region Department of Education, Edinburgh: Moray House Institute

Draper, J. and McMichael, P. (1996) 'I am the eye of the needle and everything passes through me', *School Organisation*, Vol. 16, No. 2, pp. 149–63

Draper, J. and McMichael, P. (1998a) 'Preparing a profile: likely applicants for primary headship', *Educational Management and Administration*, Vol. 26, No. 2, pp. 161–72

Draper, J. and McMichael, P. (1998b) 'Making sense of primary headship', *School Leadership and Management*, Vol. 18, No. 2, pp. 197–211

Draper, J. and McMichael, P. (1998c) 'In the firing line?: the attractions of secondary headship', *Management in Education*, Vol. 12, No. 2, pp. 15–20

Draper, J. and McMichael, P. (2000) 'Contextualising new headship', *School Leadership and Management*, Vol. 20, No. 4, pp. 459–73

Draper, J. and McMichael, P. (2002) 'Managing acting headship: a safe pair of hands', *School Leadership and Management*, Vol. 22, No. 3, pp. 289–303

Draper, J. and McMichael, P. (2003) 'Keeping the show on the road: the role of the acting headteacher', *Educational Management and Administration*, Vol. 31, No. 1, pp. 67–81

Duignan, P. (2001) 'The Managed Heart', *Improving Schools*, Vol. 4, pp. 33–9

Duignan, P. and Collins, V. (2001) 'Leadership challenges in frontline service organisations', paper delivered at British Educational Research Association Annual Conference, Leeds

Earley, P., Evans, J., Collarbone, P., Gold, G. and Halpin, D. (2001) *Establishing the Current State of School Leadership in England*, Institute of Education: University of London

Ehrich, L., Cranston, N. and Kimber, M. (2006) 'Ethical dilemmas: the "bread and butter" of educational leaders' lives', *Journal of Educational Administration*, Vol. 44, No. 3, pp. 106–21

Eraut, M. (1994) *Developing Professional Knowledge and Competence*, London: Falmer Press

Fullan, M. (2001) *Leading in a Culture of Change*, San Francisco: Jossey-Bass

Gardner, H. (1995) *Leading Minds: An Anatomy of Leadership*, London: HarperCollins

Garrett, V. and McGeachie, B. (1999) 'Preparation for headship ? The role of the deputy head in the primary school', *School Leadership and Management*, Vol. 19, No. 1, pp. 67–81

General Teaching Council Scotland (GTCS), gtcs.org.uk (accessed 1 August 2008)

Grace, G. (2002) *Catholic Schools: Mission, Markets and Morality*, London: Routledge Falmer

Goleman, D. (2000) 'Leadership that gets results', *Harvard Business Review*, March/April, pp. 78–90

Graham, J. W. (1988) 'Transformational leadership: fostering follower autonomy, not automatic followership', in Hunt, J. G., Baglia, B. R., Dachler, H. P. and Schriesheim, C. A. (eds) (1988) *Emerging Leadership Vistas*, Lexington MA: Lexington Books, pp. 73–9

Grant, M. (1995) 'High hopes or hemlock: quality assurance in Highland Region', in Knowles, I. and Wight, J. (eds) (1995) *High Hopes or Hemlock? Assuring Quality in Schools*, Edinburgh: Moray House Publications

Granville, S. (2003) *Evaluation of Heads Together Pilot Project*. Edinburgh: SEED (online). Available from URL: www.scotland.gov.uk/Publications/2003/09/18122/26042 (accessed 1 August 2008)

Green, M. (1999) 'The local governance of education: a political perspective', in Bryce, T. and Humes, W. (eds) (1999) *Scottish Education*, first edn, Edinburgh: Edinburgh University Press, pp. 146–51

Gronn, P. (1999) 'Substituting for leadership: the neglected role of the leadership couple', *Leading and Managing*, Vol. 4, No. 4, pp. 294–318

Gronn, P. (2000) 'Distributed properties', *Educational Management and Administration*, Vol. 28, No. 3, pp. 317–88

Gronn, P. (2003) *The New Work of Educational Leaders*, London: Paul Chapman

Gunter, H. M. (2001) *Leaders and Leadership in Education*, London: Paul Chapman

Gunter, H. M. (2005) *Leading Teachers*, London: Continuum

Halpin, D. (2001) 'Hope, utopianism and educational management', *Cambridge Journal of Education*, Vol. 31, No. 1, pp. 103–18

Hamilton, L. (2002) 'Constructing pupil identity: personhood and ability', *The British Educational Research Journal*, Vol. 28, pp. 591–602

Handy, C. (1991) *The Age of Unreason*, London: Century Business

Hargreaves, D. and Hopkins, D. (1991) *The Empowered School: The Management and Practice of Development Planning*, London: Cassell

Harris, A. (2002) *School Improvement: What's in it for Schools?*, London: Routledge Falmer

Hay McBer (2000) *The Lessons of Leadership*, London: Hay Management Consultants

Hayes, J. and Nutman, P. (1981) *Understanding the Unemployed: The Psychological Effects of Unemployment*, London: Tavistock

Health and Safety Executive/ACAS (2004) *Stress at Work*, London: HSE

Hellawell, D. (1991) 'The changing role of the head in the primary school in England', *School Organisation*, Vol. 11, No. 3, pp. 321–38

Henderson, D. (2002) 'HMI share blame over 5–14 overload', *Times Educational Supplement Scotland*, 8 November

HMI (1984) *Learning and Teaching in Scottish Secondary Schools: School Management*, Edinburgh: HMSO

HMI (1988) *Effective Secondary Schools*, Edinburgh: HMSO

HMI (1989) *Effective Primary Schools*, Edinburgh: HMSO

HMIE (2007a) *How Good Is Our School* (version 3) (online). Available from URL: www.hmie.gov.uk/documents/publication/hgiosjte3.html (accessed 1 August 2008)

HMIE (2007b) 'Leadership for learning: the challenges of leading in a time of change', Livingston: HMIE (online). Available from URL: www.hmie.gov.uk/Publications.aspx (accessed 1 August 2008)

HMIE (2008a) 'HMIE INEA Inspections' (online). Available from URL: www.hmie.gov.uk/AboutUs/InspectionResources/INEA (accessed 1 August 2008)

HMIE (2008b) 'Leadership Coaching Project' (Moray Council, Coaching for Change Project) (online). Available from URL: www.hmie.gov.uk/GoodPractice/Materials.aspx?theme=24&topic=132 (accessed 1 August 2008)

Hochschild, S. R. (1983) *The Managed Heart: Commercialisation of Human Feeling*, Los Angeles: University of California Press

Hopkins, D., Harris, A. and Jackson, D. (1997) 'Understanding the school's capacity for development: growth states and strategies', *School Leadership and Management*, Vol. 17, pp. 401–11

Howson, J. (2002) 'And the consequence is', *Times Educational Supplement*, 22 November, p. 29

Humes, W. (1986) *The Leadership Class in Scottish Education*, Edinburgh: John Donald

Jamieson, C. (2002) Keynote Address at The Edinburgh Conference, Edinburgh

Jones, A. (1987) *Leadership for Tomorrow's Schools*, London: Basil Blackwell

Jones, N. (1999) 'The changing role of the school head', *Educational Management and Administration*, Vol. 27, No. 4, pp. 441–51

Kakabadse, A. and Kakabadse, N. (1999) *Essence of Leadership*, London: International Thompson Business Press

Kelly, G. (1980)'A Study of the Manager's Orientation towards the Transition from Work to Retirement', unpublished PhD thesis, University of Leeds

Kerr, J. (1992) *Management Training for Headteachers: An Evaluation Report*, Edinburgh: Lothian Regional Council Education Dept

Kirk, G. (2000) *Enhancing Quality in Teacher Education*, Edinburgh: Dunedin Academic Press

Kolb, D. (1984) *Experiential Learning: Experience as a Source of Learning and Development*, Englewood Cliffs, NJ: Prentice Hall

Kotter, J.P. (1996) *Leading Change*, Boston MA: Harvard Business School Press

Landon, J. (1995) 'In-service and professional development: the emergence of post-graduate award schemes', in O'Brien, J. (ed.) (1995) *Current Changes and Challenges in European Teacher Education: SCOTLAND*, Bruxelles: Moray House Institute of Education Professional Development Centre in association with COMPARE-TE European Network

Law, S. and Glover, D. (2000) *Educational Leadership and Learning*, Buckingham: Open University Press

Leithwood, K., Jantzi, D. and Steinbach, R. (1999) *Changing Leadership for Changing Times*, Buckingham: Open University Press

Leithwood, K.J., Jantzi, D. and Steinbach, R. (2000) *Understanding Schools as Intelligent Systems*, Stamford: JAI Press

Louis, H. R. (1980) 'Surprise and sensemaking', *Administrative Science Quarterly*, Vol. 25, pp. 226–51

MacBeath, J. (ed.) (1998) *Effective School Leadership: Responding to Change*, London: Paul Chapman

MacBeath, J. and Mortimore, P. (eds) (2001) *Improving School Effectiveness*, Buckingham: Open University Press

MacBeath, J. and Myers, K. (1999) *Effective School Leaders*, London: Prentice Hall

McConnell, J. (2002) Interview in Glasgow *Sunday Herald*, 10 November, p. 12

MacGilchrist, B., Myers K. and Reed, J. (2004) *The Intelligent School*, second edn, London: Sage

Mackenzie, H. (1995) *Craigroyston Days: The Story of an Educational Revolution*, Edinburgh: Mainstream

McPherson, A. and Raab, C. (1988) *Governing Education: A Sociology of Policy*, Edinburgh: Edinburgh University Press

Malcolm, H. and Schlapp, U. (1997) *5–14 in the Primary School: A Continuing Challenge*, Edinburgh: Scottish Council for Research in Education

Malcolm, H. and Wilson, V. (2000) *The Price of Quality: An Evaluation of the Costs of the SQH programme*, Edinburgh: Scottish Council for Research in Education

Management Charter Initiative (MCI) (1991) Management Standards Implementation Pack, London: MCI

McPherson, A. and Raab, C. D. (1988) *Governing Education: A Sociology of Policy since 1945*, Edinburgh: Edinburgh University Press

Mercer, D. (1996) 'Can they walk on water? Professional isolation and the secondary headteacher', *School Leadership and Management*, Vol. 16, No. 2, pp. 165–78

Menter, I., Muschamp, Y., Nichols, P., Pollard, A. and Ozga, J. (1995) 'Still carrying the can: primary school headship in the 1990s', *School Organisation*, Vol. 15, No. 3, pp. 301–12

Menter, I., Holligan, C., Mthenjwa, V. (2005) 'Reaching the parts that need to be reached? the impact of the Scottish Qualification for Headship', *School Leadership and Management*, Vol. 25, No. 1, pp. 7–23

Menter, I., Holligan, C., Mthenjwa, V. and Hair, M. (2003) *Heading for Success: The Evaluation of the Scottish Qualification for Headship*, Edinburgh: Scottish Executive Education Department

Mercer, D. (1996) 'Can they walk on water ? Professional isolation and the secondary headteacher', *School Leadership and Management*, Vol. 16, No. 2, pp. 165–78

Moller, J. (1996) 'Reframing educational leadership in the perspective of dilemmas', in Jacobson, S., Hickcox, E. and Stevenson, R. (eds) (1996) *School Administration: Persistent Dilemmas in Preparation and Practice*, Westport, CN: Praeger, pp. 207–26

Moos, L. and Dempster, N. (1998) 'Some comparative learnings from the study', in MacBeath, J. (ed.) (1998) *Effective School Leadership: Responding to Change*, London:

Paul Chapman

Morley, L. and Razool, N. (1999) *School Effectiveness: Fracturing the Discourse*, London: Falmer Press

Morris, B. and Reeves, J. (2000) 'Implementing the national Qualification for Headship in Scotland: (a) critical reflection', *Journal of In-service Education*, Vol. 26, No. 3, pp. 517–31

Morrison, K. (2002) *School Leadership and Complexity Theory*, London: Routledge Falmer

Mulford, B. and Sillins, H. (2001) 'Leadership for organisational learning and improved student outcomes – what do we know?', *NSIN Research Matters*, Vol. 15, pp. 1–8

Murphy, D. (2002) 'Dilemmas of practice in leading Scottish comprehensive schools', paper delivered at CCEAM Conference, Umea, Sweden

Murphy, D. (2003a) 'Scottish heads/deputes survey – May 2003: a summary report, *Bylines* (Journal of the Headteachers Association of Scotland) Vol. 17, No. 3, p. 23

Murphy, D. (2003b) *Changing Roles and Workload among Secondary School Heads/ Deputes in Scotland*, CEL Paper, Edinburgh: Centre for Educational Leadership, The University of Edinburgh

Murphy, D. (2003c) Signs of progress ... but there's room for improvement – secondary school leaders' attitudes to some current Scottish policy concerns. CEL Paper, Edinburgh: Centre for Educational Leadership, The University of Edinburgh

Murphy, D. (2007) *Professional School Leadership – Dealing with Dilemmas*, Edinburgh: Dunedin Academic Press

Murphy, D., Draper, J., O'Brien, J. and Cowie, M. (2002a) 'Local management of the Scottish Qualification for Headship (SQH)', *Journal of In-service Education*, Vol. 28, No. 2, pp. 277–95

Murphy, D., O'Brien, J., Draper, J. and Cowie, M. (2002b) 'Education authority co-ordination of the Scottish Qualification for Headship', Edinburgh: Faculty of Education, The University of Edinburgh

Murphy, J. (1991) *Restructuring Schools: Capturing and Assessing the Phenomena*, New York: Teachers College Press

Murphy, J. (1992) *The Landscape of Leadership Preparation: Reframing the Education of School Administrators*, Newbury Park, CA: Corwin Press

Murphy, J. (1998) 'Preparation for the school principalship: the United States experience', *School Leadership and Management*, Vol. 18, No. 3, pp. 359–72

Murphy, J. (2002) 'Re-culturing the profession of educational leadership: new blueprints', *Education Administration Quarterly*, Vol. 38, pp. 176–91

Murray, J. (ed.) (2002) *Building on Success: Case Studies of Ethos Award Winners 1997–2001*, Edinburgh: Scottish Schools Ethos Network

National College for School Leadership (NCSL), www.ncsl.org.uk/ (accessed 1 August 2008)

National College for School Leadership (NCSL) (2008) 'Find a programme' (online). Available from URL: www.ncsl.org.uk/programmes-index.htm (accessed 1 August 2008)

National CPD Team (2005a) 'The contribution of chartered teachers, advice and guidance' (online). Available from URL: www.ltscotland.org.uk/cpdscotland/about/background. asp (accessed 1 August 2008)

National CPD Team (2005b) 'Headteacher appointment procedures' (online). Available from URL: www.ltscotland.org.uk/cpdscotland/about/background.asp (accessed 1 August 2008)

National Debate (2003) (online). Available from URL: www.scotland.gov.uk/News/ Releases/2003/01/3009 (accessed 1 August 2008)

National Priorities, Scotland (online). Available from URL: www.ltscotland.org.uk/ cpdscotland/nationalpriorities.asp (accessed 1 August 2008)

Nicholson, N. and West, M. (1988) *Managerial Job Change: Men and Women in Transition*,

Cambridge: Cambridge University Press

O'Brien, J. (2000) *Scottish Qualification for Headship – Unit 4:Leadership and Management 'Assessment and Extended Simulation' Development, Trial and Training.* Report (mimeograph) for SQH National Advisory Group, Edinburgh: Faculty of Education: The University of Edinburgh

O'Brien, J. and Draper, J. (2001) 'Developing effective school leaders? Initial views of the Scottish Qualification for Headship (SQH)', *Journal of In-service Education*, Vol. 27, No. 1, pp. 109–21

O'Brien, J. and Murphy, D. (2003) 'Assessing effective interpersonal skills in prospective school leaders', *Journal of In-service Education*, Vol. 29, No. 2, pp. 221–35

O'Brien, J. and MacLeod, G. (forthcoming) *The Social Agenda of the School*, Edinburgh: Dunedin Academic Press

O'Brien, J. and Torrance, D. (2005) 'Professional learning for school principals: developments in Scotland', *Education Research and Perspectives*, Vol. 32, No. 2, pp. 165–81

OECD (2004) *Education at a Glance*, Paris: OECD

OECD (2007) *Improving School Leadership – OECD background report: Scotland*, Edinburgh: SEED

OECD (2008) *Reviews of National Policies for Education: Quality and Equity of Schooling in Scotland*, Paris: OECD

Office for Standards in Education (1998) *The Annual Report of Her Majesty's Chief Inspector of Schools: Standards and Quality in Education 1996/9*, London: HMSO

Online Communities (2008) www.ltscotland.org.uk/onlinecommunities/login.asp (accessed 1 August 2008)

Paterson, L. (2000a) *Education and the Scottish Parliament*, Edinburgh: Dunedin Academic Press

Paterson, L. (2000b) *Crisis in the Classroom*, Edinburgh: Mainstream

Paterson, L. (2002) 'Don't put them in a class of their own', *Edinburgh Evening News*, 18 October

Ranson, S. (1994) *Towards the Learning Society*, London: Cassell

Reeves, J., Mahony, P. and Moos, L. (1997) 'Headship: issues of career', *Teacher Development*, Vol. 1, No. 1, pp. 43–56

Reeves, J., Forde, C., Casteel, V. and Lynas, R. (1998) 'Developing a model of practice: designing a framework for the professional development of school leaders and managers', *School Leadership and Management*, Vol. 18, No. 2, pp. 185–96

Reeves, J., Morris, B., Forde, C. and Turner, E. (2001) 'Exploring the impact of continuing professional development on practice in the context of the Scottish Qualification for Headship', *Journal of In-Service Education*, Vol. 27, No. 2, pp. 203–20

Reeves, J., Forde, C., O'Brien, J., Smith, P. and Tomlinson, H. (2002) *Performance Management in Education: Improving Practice*, London: Paul Chapman Publishing in association with BELMAS

Renfrew Council (2002) 'Renfrew', *Times Educational Supplement*, 8 November

Ribbins, P. and Gunter, H. (2002) 'Mapping leadership studies in education: towards a typology of knowledge domains', *Educational Management and Administration*, Vol. 30, pp. 359–85

Ribbins, P. and Marland, M. (1994) *Headship Matters*, Harlow: Longman

Riddell, S. and Brown, S. (eds) (1991) *School Effectiveness Research: Its Messages for School Improvement*, SOED, Edinburgh: HMSO

Riley, K.A. (1998a) 'Creating the leadership climate', *International Journal of Leadership in Education*, Vol. 1, No. 2, pp. 137–53

Riley, K. (1998b) *Whose School is it Anyway?*, London: Falmer Press

Rost, J. C. (1998) 'Leadership and management', in Hickman, G. R. (ed.) (1998) *Leading Organizations: Perspectives for a New Era*, London: Sage

Samier, E. (2002) 'Weber on education and its administration: prospects for leadership in a rationalised world', *Educational Management and Administration*, Vol. 30, pp. 27–45

Sammons, P., Hillman, J. and Mortimore, P. (1995) *Key Characteristics of Effective Schools: A Review of School Effectiveness*. Research for the Office of Standards in Education, London: OFSTED

Schein, E. H. (1985) *Organizational Culture and Leadership*, San Francisco: Jossey-Bass

Scobbie, J. (1984) *The School Experience*, Airdrie: J. K. Scobbie

Scottish Executive (2001) 'St Modan's – an example worth following: McConnell', press release, 13 March (online). Available from URL: www.scotland.gov.uk/News/Releases/2001/03/80d7e76b-f7a3-4afb-86bc-7c2c906517fb (accessed 1 August 2008)

Scottish Executive (2003) 'National Debate on Education', press release, 29 January (online). Available from URL: www.scotland.gov.uk/News/Releases/2003/01/3009) (accessed 1 August 2008)

Scottish Executive (2007) Concordat between the Scottish Government and local government (online). Available from URL: www.scotland.gov.uk/Publications/2007/11/13092240/concordat (accessed 1 August 2008)

Scottish Executive Education Department (SEED) (2000a) Standards in Scotland's Schools etc Act, Edinburgh: HMSO

Scottish Executive Education Department (2000b) *A Teaching Profession for the 21ˢᵗ Century* (The report of the Committee of Inquiry into the professional conditions of service of teachers: the McCrone Report), Edinburgh: SEED

Scottish Executive Education Department (2001a) A Teaching Profession for the 21ˢᵗ Century (the Agreement based on the McCrone Report) (online). Available from URL: www.scotland.gov.uk/library3/education/ tp21a–03.asp (accessed 1 August 2008)

Scottish Executive Education Department (2001b) Circular 3/2001, *Guidance on flexibility in the curriculum* (online). Available from URL: www.scotland.gov.uk/Publications/2001/09/10025/File-1 (accessed 1 August 2008)

Scottish Executive Education Department (2003a) *Educating for Excellence – Choice and Opportunity: The Executive's Response to the National Debate*. Edinburgh: SEED (online). Available from URL: www.scotland.gov.uk/Publications/2003/01/16226/17176 (accessed 1 August 2008)

Scottish Executive Education Department (2003b) *Continuing Professional Development for Educational Leaders*, Edinburgh: SEED

Scottish Executive Education Department (2004) *A Curriculum for Excellence*, Edinburgh: SEED (online). Available from URL: www.scotland.gov.uk/Topics/Education/Schools/curriculum/ACE (accessed 1 August 2008)

Scottish Executive Education Department (2005a) *Ambitious, Excellent Schools: Leadership – A Discussion Paper* (online). Available from URL: www.scotland.gov.uk/Publications/2005/06/17104251/42555 (accessed 1 August 2008)

Scottish Executive Education Department (2005b) *Ambitious, Excellent Schools: Standard for Headship? A Consultation Paper* (online). Available from URL: www.scotland.gov.uk/Publications/2005/06/17104149/41519 (accessed 1 August 2008)

Scottish Executive Education Department (2005c) *Ambitious, Excellent Schools: Standard for Headship – November 2005* (online). Available from URL: www.scotland.gov.uk/Publications/2005/11/3085829/58300#2 (accessed 1 August 2008)

Scottish Executive Education Department(2006a) Scottish Schools (Parental Involvement) Act (online). Available from URL: www.opsi.gov.uk/legislation/scotland/acts2006/asp_20060008_en_1 (accessed 1 August 2008)

Scottish Executive Education Department (2006b) *Getting It Right for Every Child: Implementation Plan* (online). Available from URL: www.scotland.gov.uk/Resource/Doc/131460/0031397.pdf (accessed 1 August 2008)

Scottish Executive Education Department (2006c) *Achieving the Standard for Headship – Providing Choice and Alternatives: A Consultation Document* (online). Available from URL: www.scotland.gov.uk/Publications/2006/01/31093326/0) (accessed 1 August 2008)

Scottish Executive Education Department (2008) The Parental Involvement in Headteacher and Deputy Headteacher Appointments (Scotland) Regulations 2007, Scottish Statutory Instruments 2007 No. 132 (online). Available from URL: www.opsi.gov.uk/legislation/scotland/ssi2007/ssi_20070132_en_1 (accessed 1 August 2008)

Scottish Executive Education Department (2008) *Curriculum for Excellence: Building the Curriculum 3: A Framework for Learning and Teaching* (online). Available from URL: www.scotland.gov.uk/Publications/2008/06/06104407/3 (accessed 1 August 2008)

Scottish Government (known as Scottish Executive to 2007), www.scotland.gov.uk/home (accessed 1 August 2008)

Scottish Office (1998) New Community Schools Prospectus (online). Available from URL: www.scotland.gov.uk/library/documents-w3/ncsp-00.htm (accessed 1 August 2008)

Scottish Office Education Department (1986) *Report of the Committee of Inquiry into the Pay and Conditions of Service of School Teachers in Scotland* (The Main Report) Edinburgh: SOED

Scottish Office Education Department (1990) *Management Training for Headteachers*, Edinburgh: SOED

Scottish Office Education and Industry Department (1997) *Proposals for Developing a Scottish Qualification for Headteachers*, Consultation Document, Edinburgh: SOEID

Scottish Office Education and Industry Department (1998a) *Proposals for Developing a Framework for Continuing Professional Development for the Teaching Profession in Scotland*, Consultation Document. Edinburgh: SOEID

Scottish Office Education and Industry Department (1998b) *The Standard for Headship in Scotland*. Stirling: SQH Development Unit

Scottish Parliament, www.scottish.parliament.uk/ (accessed 1 August 2008)

Scottish Parliament (2008) Minutes of Proceedings, 30 January (online). Available from URL: www.scottish.parliament.uk/business/chamber/mop-08/mop08-01-30.htm (accessed 1 August 2008)

Scottish Qualification for Headship (2008) 'The SQH programme' (online). Available from URL: www.sqh.ed.ac.uk/programme (accessed 1 August 2008)

Scottish Schools Ethos Network, www.ethosnet.co.uk (accessed 1 August 2008)

Selznick, P. (1957) *Leadership in Administration: A Sociological Interpretation*, Evanston, IL: Row, Peterson

Sergiovanni, T. (1992) *Moral Leadership*, San Francisco: Jossey-Bass

Sergiovanni, T. (1994) *Building Community in Schools*, San Francisco: Jossey-Bass

Sergiovanni, T. J. (2001) *Leadership: What's in it for Schools?*, London: Routledge Falmer

Southworth, G. (1990) Leadership, headship and effective primary schools, *School Organisation*, Vol. 10, No. 1, pp. 29–47

Southworth, G. (1995a) *Looking into Primary Headship: A Research Based Interpretation*, London: Falmer Press

Southworth, G. (1995b) *Talking Heads: Voices of Experience; an Investigation into Primary Headship in the 1990s*, Cambridge: Cambridge University Press

Southworth, G. (1998) *Leading Improving Primary Schools*, London, Falmer Press

Southworth, G. (2005) 'Learning-centred leadership', in Davies, B. (ed.) (2005) *The Essentials of School Leadership*, London: Paul Chapman, pp. 75–92

Stoll, L. (1999) 'Realising our potential: understanding and developing capacity for lasting improvement', *School Effectiveness and School Improvement*, Vol. 10, pp. 503–32

Stoll, L. and Fink, D. (1996) *Changing Our Schools*, Buckingham: Open University Press

Strathclyde Regional Council (1986) *Managing Progress*, Glasgow: SRC

Teacher Training Agency (1995a) *Headteachers' Leadership and Management Programme*, London: TTA

Teacher Training Agency (1995b) *National Standards for Headteachers*, London: TTA

Teacher Training Agency (1998) *TTA National Leadership Programme for Serving*

Headteachers, London: TTA

Thody, A. M. (2000) 'Followers and leaders', paper delivered at British Education, Leadership, Management and Administration Society Annual Conference, Leeds: BELMAS

Thomson, P., Blackmore, J., Sachs, J. and Tregenza, K. (2003) 'High stakes principalship –sleepless nights, heart attacks and sudden death accountabilities: reading media representations of the United States principal shortage', *Australian Journal of Education*, Vol. 47, No. 2, pp. 118–32

Thorburn. G. (2002) 'Management Structures in Schools', keynote address delivered at the Inaugural Conference of the Centre for Educational Leadership, University of Edinburgh, Airdrie

TES (2004) 'GTC returns to the fray over qualifications for headship', *Times Educational Supplement Scotland*, 17 September

Tomlinson, H., Gunter, H. and Smith, P. (eds) (1999) *Living Headship: Voices, Values and Vision*, London: Paul Chapman

Torrington, D. and Weightman, J. (1989) *The Reality of School Management*, Oxford: Blackwell Education

Ungoed-Thomas, J. (1997) *Vision of a School*, London: Cassell

Wallace, M. and Hall, V. (1994) *Inside the SMT: Teamwork in Secondary School Management*, London: Paul Chapman

Wallace, M. and Huckman, L. (1996) 'Senior management teams in large primary schools: a headteacher's solution to the complexities of post-reform management?', *School Organisation*, Vol. 16, No. 3, pp. 309–23

Watkin, C. (2000) 'The Leadership Programme for Serving Headteachers: probably the world's largest leadership development programme', *The Leadership and Organization Development Journal*, Vol. 21, No. 1, pp. 13–19

Webb, R. and Vulliamy, G. (1996) 'A deluge of directives: conflict between collegiality and managerialism in the post ERA primary school', *British Educational Research Journal*, Vol. 22, No. 4, pp. 441–58

West-Burnham, J. (1997) *Managing Quality in Schools*, London: Pitman

Williams, T. (2001) *Unrecognized Exodus, Unaccepted Accountability*, Working Paper 24, School of Policy Studies, Ontario: Queens University

Williams, T. (2003) 'Ontario's principal scarcity: yesterday's abdicated responsibility – today's unrecognised challenge', *Australian Journal of Education*, Vol. 47, No. 2, pp. 159–71

Wilson, V. and McPake, J. (1999) 'Headteachers of small Scottish primary schools', *Scottish Educational Review*, Vol. 31, No. 1, pp. 35–47

Wong, K. C. (2001) 'What kind of leaders do we need? The Case of Hong Kong', *International Studies in Educational Administration*, Vol. 29, No. 2, pp. 2–12

INDEX